Colin Macdonald

Chronicles of Stratheden, a Highland parish of to-day

Colin Macdonald

Chronicles of Stratheden, a Highland parish of to-day

ISBN/EAN: 9783337157425

Printed in Europe, USA, Canada, Australia, Japan

Cover: Foto ©ninafisch / pixelio.de

More available books at **www.hansebooks.com**

CHRONICLES OF STRATHEDEN

A HIGHLAND PARISH
OF TO-DAY

BY

A RESIDENT

WILLIAM BLACKWOOD AND SONS
EDINBURGH AND LONDON
MDCCCLXXXI

CONTENTS.

CHAP.		PAGE
	INTRODUCTION, ...	1
I.	THE CROFTERS OF A HIGHLAND PARISH OF TO-DAY, ...	9
II.	RELIGION OF A HIGHLAND PARISH OF TO-DAY, ...	33
III.	THE POLITICS OF A HIGHLAND PARISH OF TO-DAY, ...	66
IV.	LANGUAGE AND LITERATURE IN A HIGHLAND PARISH OF TO-DAY, . .	85
V.	MANSES AND MINISTERS IN A HIGHLAND PARISH OF TO-DAY, . . .	103
VI.	HEATHFIELD HOUSE AND THE PEOPLE'S FRIEND, ...	126
VII.	POPULAR ENTERTAINMENTS AND AMUSEMENTS IN A HIGHLAND PARISH OF TO-DAY, ...	144

CONTENTS.

VIII. SHOPKEEPING IN A HIGHLAND PARISH OF TO-DAY, ... 181

IX. THE HOME AND SURROUNDINGS OF A "BIG FAIRMER" IN A HIGHLAND PARISH OF TO-DAY, ... 202

X. THE USUAL VISITORS TO A HIGHLAND PARISH, ... 229

XI. BIG DAYS IN A HIGHLAND PARISH, . 256

XII. CONCLUSION, ... 266

CHRONICLES OF STRATHEDEN.

INTRODUCTION.

IT is the aim of the writer of the following pages to sketch a Highland parish of our own times, just as it is; and in doing this, there will be made such references to the past as may enable the reader, to some extent at least, to compare a Highland parish of to-day with that of a past of from twenty to forty years ago.

While there is little or nothing sensational to chronicle, it is hoped that these sketches will not be lacking in interest to such as care to glance at the changes that have taken place within recent years, in a part of the country long, on account of its remoteness, invested with a sort of romance, and now largely frequented by many, not only for the invigorating benefit of its bracing air, but also for the richness and variety of its natural scenery.

Stratheden is a fairly representative Highland parish, and possesses the interesting features of being at once materially influenced by the changes of recent times, and of retaining a few of the special characteristics of a Highland parish of other days.

Though not a sound particularly inviting to the lover of harmony, the whistle of a passing railway train may now be heard along with the bleating of the sheep that pasture on the hillsides of Stratheden; and those of the inhabitants who can, from personal knowledge, compare the present with the past of twenty years ago, reckon this fact alone as a marked sign of the progress of the age, and as a patent enough proof that the *remoteness* of the past has vanished.

There are many yet living who remember a time when Stratheden was essentially remote in respect of the limited means of communication between it and the larger world outside. A journey from Stratheden to Glasgow or Edinburgh, not very many years ago, occupied four days, and such a journey was then thought as great an undertaking as a journey across the Atlantic is considered by many in the present day. Railway trains were unknown, and telegraphic communication undreamt of. The mail-coach was the principal means of communication; and though it was tardy, compared with the rapid travelling of to-day, there are many—and these by no means slow people—not ashamed to look back with a sort of fond regret on the days of the mail-coach. No doubt there were many bleak journeys,—days and nights when drifting snow or pelting rain had to be encountered; but, generally speaking, these uninviting experiences were soon forgot, and there was a kind of pleasing excitement in the halting at the stages on the way, the chattings as the travellers *walked* up the steep brae, and the rest in the cosy best room of the wayside inn. Along with all this, the coaching days possessed another feature which many, probably with a sigh, will feel as an advantage indeed. There was not, as a rule, that exhausting excitement which the very rapidity and haste of to-day so much, and, it is to be feared, so injuriously occasion. Time then, as now, perhaps, was money; and though people took more time—or, as the disciples of the modern estimate of proper travelling may think, *lost* more time—the older generation managed to get along wonderfully well, and we are not sure that money, relatively that is to say, was not as plentiful as it is to-day. Be this as it may, our travelling, in its means and its rapidity, is widely different from that of the period alluded to. London is within twenty-four hours of Stratheden; and as for Glasgow or Edinburgh, not very long ago literally far away, they are to-day considered to be at the very door. The whistle of a railway train several times a-day echoes along the glens of Stratheden, and the telegraphic wire is at hand to flash its message at any moment at the bidding of the wondering inhabitants. A letter posted in London on the evening of one day may be read in Stratheden next evening; and now that so many sportsmen and tourists, having important interests to attend to in the great metropolis and other places, frequent districts as far away as Stratheden, such facilities of communication must be of immense value. No doubt many persons, on the other hand, may luxuriate in the quiet retreat afforded by places like Stratheden, happy in the thought of getting away "from the madding crowd," away from the anxious worry of a busy life with its letters and telegrams; but where, as is sometimes the case, the interests far away must be kept in hand in the quiet Highland straths and glens, the benefits of train and telegraphs must be highly prized. There was a time, about thirty years ago, when letters came but once a-week to Stratheden, and that by a circuitous and tedious route. Letters were not then so numerous as they are now; and as for newspapers, not more than half-a-dozen copies came to the parish, though the population was as large then as at present. At this moment letters arrive thrice daily in Stratheden; and, judging from the bulk of the postman's bag as he passes along the strath, it excites a little wonder to think of the large number of letters that constantly come to our peaceful solitudes. The increase in the number of newspapers is equally remarkable. Instead of half-a-dozen copies, to-day fully fourteen dozen, including weekly and daily papers, regularly come to the parish, all duly subscribed for.

The same element of change is apparent with reference to the garb popularly understood to be worn by the native Highlander, and with regard to the language so long spoken in so many of our Highland parishes—indeed, the only language used by the great majority of the inhabitants of a Highland parish of some forty years ago. However commonly it may have been used in other days, the philabeg (kilt) cannot be said to have been in general use at any period within the last fifty years. Twenty years ago three-fourths of the school-boys in a Highland parish were kilted loons, and many of them continued to wear the kilt until they were close on twenty years of age. To-day, taking an average Highland public school, we look in vain for even one in five wearing the ancient garb—a fact suggestive enough of the slender likelikood of its ever again becoming the popular costume.

And so with the Gaelic language. The use of it too, beyond all dispute, is dying out; and much as many of us may regret it, the time cannot be far distant when, even in the remotest Highland parish, Gaelic accents will be rare indeed.

Another marked change in a Highland parish of the present day is visible in the greatly improved aspect of the dwelling-houses. The houses as they now are, with very few exceptions, bear little or no resemblance to those of, say, forty years ago, —and even within the last fifteen years a somewhat marked change in this respect has taken place. No small proportion of the homes of the people have within the latter period been converted from earthen-walled, heather-thatched, imperfectly-lighted, badly-ventilated habitations, into substantially-built, stone-walled, slated, well-lighted, well-ventilated, and neat-looking cottages. No doubt from beneath the sooty ceiling of the humble unpretending hut of other days there frequently emerged as true, good people, and as successful in the larger world outside, as ever sat in spacious gorgeously-furnished dwellings; but this does not alter the fact that there was room for improvement in the matter of both architectural design and internal comfort. The thatched roof of other days, composed of earth and heather, is now rapidly giving way to the slated roof, though the former type—the earth-and-heather structure—enjoys a lingering existence among the crofter-fishermen on the western seaboard of the counties of Ross, Sutherland, and Inverness. The proprietor of Stratheden, and many other Highland lairds, desirous to promote the comfort of the crofters, give considerable material encouragement to house-improvement by supplying wood and lime, the crofters themselves having thus to provide slates and labour only, which most of them are able, and all willing, to provide.

For obvious reasons, the *names* employed in the

following pages are fictitious, but the persons spoken of, or allowed to speak for themselves, are veritable persons well known to the author, and the beliefs and opinions set forth are such as he has heard, and hears, expressed in various Highland parishes of to-day.

CHAPTER I.

THE CROFTERS OF A HIGHLAND PARISH OF TO-DAY.

THE Highland crofter system has for some time past been receiving considerable attention. Eager theorists of the sentimental order are in this, as in other matters, apt to forget the plain teaching of facts. This is noticeable in the case of some writers in the newspapers who propound generous-looking but impracticable theories for the amelioration, as they call it, of the condition of the Highland crofter. These persons forget that the average crofter is quite satisfied with his lot. This, of course, is no reason why outsiders should not consider that there is little cause for the crofters being satisfied, or why efforts should not be made to improve the existing situation. At the same time, it is a fact worth remembering by such as recommend changes in the condition of Highland crofters. It is difficult to induce the crofter to aspire to anything better than his existing lot. There need be no pedantry in reminding the reader that happiness is a relative term, and consequently there is no reason why the average crofter should not feel as happy in his own way as any other sort of person. When the news of the diabolical attempt on the life of the Emperor of Russia in 1880 reached Stratheden, we heard a Stratheden crofter say: "Whatna' meesurable life that Emperar o' Rooshia must hev. Wi' all their grandar and riches and all *that*, some o' them big people are no happy. Oorselves is happier, though we're poor, and hesna' but oor wee hooses and bitties o' lawnd." This style of comment is quite common, and might be usefully pondered over by those who mourn over the "miseries" of Highland crofters, and propound theories of reform. Certain tourists, knowing little or nothing of the actual condition of crofters, but influenced by sentiment and afflicted with a fondness for seeing themselves in print, happen to come across a wretched-looking hut— a sorry fabric of earth and heather—such as some of the West Highland crofters continue to live in. Thinking themselves capable of showing how the supposed misery can be removed, they at once proceed to ventilate their generally crude schemes of reform. But the problem — if problem it can be really called — of the crofter system cannot be settled in this emotional and hasty fashion. Time at least is needed for removing real drawbacks. Let us now look at the general circumstances of Highland crofters.

The surroundings of the crofter are not the same in every district of the Highlands. One prominent difference must be noticed. The crofters of the eastern districts of Ross, Sutherland, and Inverness, as a rule, depend entirely on the croft; while the crofters of the western seaboard of the same counties are crofter-fishermen, depending for a living as much on the fishing as on the croft. For about half of the year these crofter-fishermen are engaged in fishing. Their boats are usually manned by six persons—five men and a boy, the latter being a sort of *multum in parvo* institution, combining the functions of cook, message-boy, and general servant. In some instances these boats are the property of one individual, the others manning the craft being hired men; but frequently the boat is a joint-stock concern, and the profits of the season's fishing are divided, share and share alike, among the joint owners. Sometimes they make a good thing of it; and it is quite common to hear of a boat's crew earning in a season one hundred and fifty pounds sterling, which, though it may have to be divided among five, represents a decidedly successful fishing. Most of these crofter-fishermen are of a saving turn. They fare simply—chiefly on fish, potatoes, milk, and meal—and rarely cultivate expensive tastes. At the same time, we have frequently heard shopkeepers in the districts where crofter-fishermen are to be met with, say that the dress fabrics ordinarily purchased by the wives and daughters of these people are of a more expensive kind than that commonly used by many in higher positions of life. Tea is a favourite beverage in most of their homes; and within recent years there has been a considerable increase in the use of the "cup that cheers." The other cup, that does more than cheer, is not, of course, universally despised; but these crofter-fishermen are, as a class, sober people.

From about the end of September until the middle of May the greater number of them are at home, during which period—harvesting is generally late in these districts—the requirements of the croft are attended to. For the rest of the year they are away at fishing-stations in Wick, Stornoway, Peterhead, and Fraserburgh. Their winter is a comparatively idle one. Some of them prosecute the ling and cod fishing; but they don't often make this a busy or prolonged work, and the principal winter work consists in threshing a few sheaves of oats or barley daily, to keep themselves in meal and their cattle in fodder. Their crofts, as a rule, are not too productive, but this is sometimes the fault of the crofter as much as of the croft. Though some crofters are too poor to expend any money in improving their crofts, there are many of them who, by the exercise of a little industry in the matter of drainage and collecting manure, might materially improve their holdings. Many of them say that if they had leases instead of the year-to-year occupancy which, with the exception of one or two districts, is the rule among these crofter-fishermen, matters would improve, because of the greater security of tenure. Besides the fact, however, that few of them wish for leases, probably fearing that increased rents would follow, it is doubtful whether leases would very materially alter their general circumstances. They lack the feeling of entire dependence on the croft, and hence the absence of a powerful motive to improve it.

The croft ordinarily consists of from three to seven acres of arable land, in addition to the right of pasture for some half-dozen head of cattle, a dozen or more sheep, and one horse. The "rent," generally speaking, is very moderate — sometimes under ten shillings an acre, though there are cases where it may be about double that figure. Some crofts can yield the annual meal requirements of the crofter's family, but many fall short of this, and some crofters have to buy considerable quantities of meal, for which, however, their fishing profits come in conveniently.

Their method of harvesting barley is peculiar. It is pulled up by the root — not, however, as some teetotallers might suspect, with thirsty designs after extracting some "barley-bree" from the uprooted stalk. It is applied to quite other purposes, — for doing, indeed, what the "barley-bree" is credited with often *undoing*—namely, *thatching* their houses, and making their homes comfortable. The barley-straw, root and all, is placed as thatch on the dwelling-house; and whatever may be thought of the general design of the house, the use to which this barley-straw is ultimately applied shows something like utilitarian leanings in the crofter *build*,— the crofter mind, we mean. Annually, as spring-time comes round, this *thatch*, enriched with the smoke of many peat-fires, is bodily removed and used for manuring the land,—so that, after all, the barley-straw arrangement by no means ends in *smoke*.

The sales off the croft, in the case of crofter-fishermen, generally speaking, are not large. Those among them that can annually sell two head of cattle, representing from £4 to £8, and about three bolls, or twelve bags, of potatoes, will reckon themselves as having had a pretty good year. A counterbalancing circumstance, however, is the often scanty return of oats and barley available for meal—the meal-purchases thus rendered necessary absorbing any profits resulting from other gains.

Some of the homes of these crofter-fishermen, as seen from without, are not suggestive of comfort, though on entering, in spite of the smoke, the irregular earthen floor, limited space, and scanty light, one is inclined to conclude that the inmates are comfortable in a way, if not happy. Several of the houses consist of an earthen wall, a roof of earth and heather, or the barley-straw alluded to, covering some half-dozen rafters—these latter of a glossy black, from long acquaintance with dense volumes of smoke "struggling to be free." Though within recent years improvements have been taking place, the internal arrangements, even to-day, are in some instances primitive enough beyond all dispute.

The floor is an earthen one; and whether because of the removing tendencies of time, or of a defect in the original construction, frequent hollows make it irregular, and render locomotion difficult to the inexperienced. The fire is in the centre of the apartment—ordinarily there are only "a but and a ben"—and whatever other comforts may be absent, there is usually sufficient warmth. Peats are plentiful; and as the moss is near at hand, scarcity of fire ordinarily means laziness. The available space is, or seems to be, limited. The windows are small—very small; and the ventilation is intrusted to the care of a bottomless barrel, or suchlike contrivance. It is only necessary, however, to remind the reader of the barley-straw arrangement to conclude that it is not specially desired that *all* the smoke should find its way through this barrel. Prominent among the furniture is what is locally called a *dresser*—a large square piece of wood, with shelves, resting on a plain table, and placed against the wall: this dresser bears a varied burden of plates, bowls, teapots, cups and saucers, jugs, spoons, knives with or without handles, as also a kettle, and one or two pots and pans.

The crofters of Stratheden are not fishermen: they depend entirely on their crofts, and their general circumstances are, in several respects, quite different from those of the crofter-fishermen we have been speaking of. Their homes, both in architectural design and internal comfort, are as a rule much superior to those of the latter; their crofts are more valuable, and the style of agriculture more advanced. Most of the crofters' houses in Stratheden are slated, and can boast of well-lighted, roomy apartments, and grates, as well as chimneys, of modern make. The croft, generally speaking, consists of from four to eight acres of arable land (in most cases very good land), with the right of "pasture" enabling the crofter to keep a horse, half-a-dozen cattle, and a few sheep. The "rents" are very moderate, and the productiveness of the croft in many instances is such that the occupier is often able, by the sale of potatoes alone, to pay his rent, and leave a surplus besides.

Iron ploughs are now common: one rarely, if ever, meets with a wooden one. A common practice in the matter of ploughing is, the average crofter having but one horse, that two neighbouring crofters enter into a joint arrangement by which the land of each is ploughed by the horses of both. What was locally considered a vast advance in the department of agriculture—a ploughing-match—

took place in Stratheden this year (1880); and being the first that ever was known among the crofter population, it naturally attracted a great deal of attention. It is quite understood that ploughing-matches will now rank among the usual and ordinary institutions of the parish.

The ordinary daily life of the average crofter in Stratheden is essentially uneventful. His ambition rarely soars beyond the monotonous routine of his immediate surroundings. Except for a few weeks in spring and autumn, his life is not a busy one. It is not one of constant toil, though, occasionally, a case may be met with where a crofter of improving tendencies gets possession of a piece of waste land to reclaim, and thus, for a time at least, he is busy enough. Winter, with most of the crofters, is a perpetual holiday. They rise late, and the principal morning requirements of the croft at this season are the letting out of the cattle and horses to water, and the doing up of the byre and stable for the day. During the day they have the oats or barley to thresh, and this is the crofter's principal winter work. Threshing-mills are unknown among the crofters generally, and, indeed, it is only within the past ten years that they have come into general use on the large farms. The steady, heavy beat of the "flail" is a familiar sound in Stratheden during the winter and spring. Sometimes the flail's duties are light. A wet harvest diminishes the number of sheaves available, and there is reason to suspect that sometimes the crop returns suffer a diminution from defective drainage or scanty manuring, or both,—defects ordinarily in the power of the crofter to remedy. The average Highland laird is very willing to grant money for drainage at a reasonable rate of interest; and the quantity of manure available might in many cases be increased by the exercise of a little care and industry during the end of autumn, and all through the winter and early spring.

The day's instalment of threshing over—and it is never hard work except when in arrear—the crofter feels he has the remainder of the day for himself, and he meditates how to spend his leisure hours. One goes to the shoemaker's shop, another to the tailor's, and a third wanders off to the smithy, while a fourth visits the shopkeeper, or "merchant," as the latter is called by many in Stratheden. The subjects and manner of conversation usual on such occasions are described in another part of this book.

The Stratheden crofter rarely goes far from home; and though railway excursion trips and other facilities for cheap travelling have modified this long-prevalent feature, there are some crofters in the parish, persons of sixty years or thereabouts, who have never travelled more than ten miles beyond Stratheden, their native parish. The younger people are getting initiated into travelling ways. Several natives of Stratheden, and like places, are in the south in various situations, and when at home, during the holiday season, their descriptions of the "big places" far away excite a curiosity which induces their untravelled brothers and sisters to see something of the world. Fairs, or as they are called in Stratheden, and in the Highlands generally, markets, constitute another attraction to the younger crofter people; and these institutions, especially those that take place only once in the year, or half-yearly, are very popular. Some parents, dubious as to the propriety of allowing their sons, and especially their daughters, to visit "them kind o' places," reply to the request of a daughter for leave to go to the market with an authoritative and peremptory refusal. "There's such an awful lot o' all kinds of people at them markets, and there's some bad people going aboot; it's no a place for young lassies at all, at all," is the reason offered for the refused permission. It seems strange, however, that in some cases the same dislike exists to allowing the young people, especially the daughters, to go to the Communion in distant parishes. Very probably it is the "awful lot o' all kinds o' people" at the Communion gathering that awakens misgivings in the parental heart, but it surely cannot be thought that the other and special portion of the paternal warning anent the market is applicable, to any great extent, to the Communion gatherings. The refusal in question is felt to be a sad deprivation, not so much because of the market itself, or even of the Communion or "Saycriemant" itself, as because of the opportunity some of the fair sex may thus lose of improving their prospects in the matrimonial market. A strict paterfamilias of the class referred to must have been a little taken aback by an observation once made to him by his daughter. Half in fun, half in earnest, he said to her: "Merran" (Marion), "am wundering you're no getting a husband; I was thinking it wull be near aboot time you was getting merrit;"—to which the daughter's reply was: "It's your own fault, father; how can I get married when you'll no let me to the market nor to the Saycriemant in other places?"!

But let us return to the crofter and his surroundings. Many of the crofts march with the "big fairmer's" ground, and this fact tended to perpetuate a sort of unpleasant feeling between the "big fairmer" and the crofter, more especially some fifteen or twenty years ago. The latter often enough was envious of the former, and the former too often selfishly indifferent about the crofter. The crofter's cattle, after the manner of most cattle, would occasionally find their way to the "big fairm," and take a more or less extensive feed of the pasture most suited to their taste. The "big fairmer," or his shepherd or other official, would send the cattle home, with a dog as convoy, and the crofter would see his cattle rushing as if for dear life, at a rattling break-neck rate, along the strath or down the hillside, and then — well, what then but what was natural in the circumstances? Why, the crofters' love for the "big fairmer" would not be increased, and the latter's murmurings about "these troublesome crofters" would grow the louder. To-day, owing to the growth of public opinion, and to the more prosaic fact of the growing use of wire-fencing, a better feeling, in this respect at least, exists between the farmers and crofters; and we are glad to chronicle that Stratheden stands creditably high with regard to cordial relations between the two classes of farmers.

Speaking of crofters there are two personages to

whom it is right to refer in passing—we mean the factor and the ground-officer. The ground-officer's duties are various, such as seeing that the crofters are cultivating their land in orthodox fashion; inquiring into disputes that may arise between neighbours about marches, rights of pasture, and the like; notifying the date of the factor's coming to the parish to collect the rents, and giving a reminder to such as may have forgot the rent-day, or otherwise neglected to pay.

The ground-officer is so far an important personage, and the factor depends a good deal for information about the crofts and other matters on his subordinate. It is understood that the ground-officer keeps a sort of daily record of crofter events, and some other matters occurring in his district, which record is submitted weekly or fortnightly, as the case may be, to the factor. It is said that other matters than such as might be supposed to come within a ground-officer's jurisdiction occasionally find, or at least used to find, their way into this official diary. We have been told that a few years ago a ground-officer in a Highland parish, in filling up his diary for a certain day, took occasion to chronicle the following item of intelligence: " Met the parish minister walking on the road to-day. *His hat was very old-looking:* he must surely have had it for a long time." While admitting the soundness of the logic with reference to the hat, it is impossible to think what this ground-officer might have inserted in his record had the parish minister met him walking elsewhere than "on the road."

The ground-officers of to-day, as a rule, are better liked than were those of other days, just because, for reasons which it is unnecessary here to mention, the feeling between the crofters and the lairds was less kindly in many cases than now, the ground-officer being viewed, of course, as the laird's local representative. To-day, matters are in every way more satisfactory. The laird and the crofters seem to understand each other better; and, though here and there a grumbler—a pretty loud one too—may be met with among the latter, for no other reason than that the laird cannot please every person, any more than other people can, a kindlier feeling, generally speaking, prevails. The ground-officer of to-day, accordingly, has more agreeable times of it, though occasionally his experiences are the reverse of pleasant. His position is in some respects a difficult one. Some crofters are too ready to think that special estate enactments must be made to meet any grievance that may crop up; and when they have stated their case to the ground-officer, for submission to the factor, if an unfavourable verdict is pronounced at headquarters, the ground-officer, as the channel of communication, comes in for no small share of the blame. The Stratheden ground-officer, Mr David Gray, is a shrewd, intelligent man, who knows his work well. He seems pretty largely endowed with the valuable quality of being "quick to hear and slow to speak," and ground-officers, like all others, will find this habit essentially useful.

The factor within whose *jurisdiction* Stratheden is situated is Mr David Pemberton. He knows as well as any can how the crofters regard him officially—that few of them fondly love him, and that many of them are prejudiced against him, simply because he is "the factor," and, perhaps, because he cannot please everybody. Mr Pemberton seems a sensible man. If, sometimes, his expression is not too amiable, it is but just to remember that the worry incident to a factor's life, the frequent and sometimes unreasonable applications made to him, and the perplexing amount of business often demanding his attention, would go far to give a sour, if not an angry, expression of countenance to persons of average capacity for amiableness. Mr Pemberton is an excellent man of business, and a straightforward man;

and whatever some of the crofters may think of him, some others in Stratheden and in neighbouring parishes, in which he acts in the same capacity, are deeply indebted to him for the valuable assistance he affords in school board and parochial board matters. He is not quite so terrible a personage as certain crofter estimates might suggest. He might perhaps cultivate the *suaviter in modo* a little more extensively, but it is not easy. So many ask him so many favours with respect to their crofts, and so many ask him so many impossible favours, that having to say "No" so often, he is apt to say it with a quite unnecessary bitterness—and, indeed, it may be, sometimes when he might have said "Yes." But he is human, as perhaps even the most prejudiced of the crofters will admit; and it is proper to remember that a just estimate of his manner necessitates a knowledge of his actual *position*, and to charitably conclude that he has his kindly feelings beneath the apparent sourness of his official face. So much for the crofters of a Highland parish of to-day, and their general surroundings.

These crofters, as a class, are a steady, law-abiding, and peace-loving people. Though in some cases not so ingenuous or truthful as might be wished, such insincerity or sneakish tendency as is met with, though to be deplored, possesses neither the depth nor the venom that would incite to deliberate opposition to law and order. They are loyal to the core, proud of their Queen and country, and entertain a sincere respect for the time-honoured institutions of the land. So far as their treatment of each other is concerned, while the rivalries of the increasing competition of to-day may render displays of envious hatred and its unworthy accompaniments more common than of yore, we still think there is an appropriateness in saying of the better type of them that—

> "Nowhere beats the heart so kindly
> As beneath the tartan plaid."

It is as difficult to forecast the future of the crofter system, as it is to see the practicableness of certain suggested schemes for the reform of real or supposed defects in the system. Rents, generally speaking, are moderate; but on the death of a crofter an increase takes place—except in the case of the widow of the deceased crofter. Assuming—which is scarcely probable, however—that the increasing process will become too great a strain on the profitableness of the croft, its fate may be easily foretold. If near a large farm, it would be added to the farm; or if far removed from such a farm, and forming one of a group of crofts, it would probably be added to another of these crofts, which would be another step in the direction of the absorption of the present crofter system into one of larger holdings. But judging from present appearances, and assuming the lairds wise and generous enough to see the reasonableness of enabling the crofter to feel he has a *home*-interest in his country, and patriotic enough to realise the usefulness of a prosperous crofter peasantry, it is not easy to believe such a result possible in the near future. And higher interests than those of the laird render it desirable that encouragement be given to a well-regulated crofter system. For various reasons it is the interest of the nation to promote it. Much as war is to be deplored, it is, of course, possible that it may be unavoidable; and those that know anything of British history must be well aware that on those battle-fields on which Britain fought most bravely, and achieved her grandest victories, no small share of the credit was due to the genuine loyalty, brave determination, and hardy endurance of her Highland soldiers. Waterloo and the Crimea are enough to instance in proof of this remark. If nowadays less is heard of the bravery and hardihood of the Highland soldier, in listening to the details of conflicts on modern battle-fields, it is not because the loyalty, the bravery, or the hardihood has vanished, but because the assimilating process so marked in recent times has so far caused the individuality of the Highlander to be merged in the national character, that the brave Highlander is known merely as the British soldier. And whence is the type of Highlander possessing such loyalty, bravery, and hardihood most likely to be procured? Unquestionably from the ranks of a healthy and prosperous crofter peasantry. May the day be far distant when Britain's honour or indignation at oppression will force her into war! But should that day come, no better soldiers could be found than the type of persons referred to. It has been so of yore. We need only mention Rannoch in Perthshire, Strathspey, Lochaber, Sutherland, Ross, and the island of Skye, as proof of what Highlanders did in other days—the latter district (Skye) contributing an unusually large number of soldiers of various ranks towards maintaining the fame of the national military greatness.

But the crofter population supplies an excellent nursery for more peaceful scenes—for more attractive spheres of life. It is well known that many of them have risen to a high place in the callings of trade and commerce, while not a few have occupied and are occupying highly respectable positions in one or other of the learned professions. Many Highland parishes might refer with pride to the success of some of their crofter youths in one or other of these spheres. We may here refer to a successful Stratheden crofter boy, Mr Alexander Irongray Cameron, a civil engineer, who, by a diligent use of his time and talents, has risen to a position of considerable eminence in his profession. He is a splendid specimen of the genuinely enlightened Highlander. Determination and perseverance are prominent features in the real Highland character. Mr Cameron is strong in these qualities, as his very successful professional career amply proves. Love of country, which includes that other patriotism which makes the true man love his native parish, is deeply rooted in Mr Cameron's heart, and no one loves Stratheden more than he does. And his affection goes further than the cheap regard of words alone. He helps with pen and purse to promote the social, intellectual, and general wellbeing of the inhabitants of his native parish. He is a true Celt—fond of the Gaelic tongue, and very unlike those weaklings that affect ignorance of, and are clearly indifferent towards, a language which, though it be disappearing, no true man will be ashamed of. Besides the material help he gives towards promoting education and general progress in the parish of Stratheden, Mr Cameron procures important situations in the south for several of the more intelligent and deserving youths of Stratheden. He is respected by all who know him. The noble laird of Stratheden, a most acute observer of character and a hater of shams, greatly respects Mr Cameron, and has more than once shown him special marks of appreciation of his good qualities and successful career. Such is a sample of what the crofter system can accomplish. No doubt Mr Cameron's career has been to some extent exceptionally successful, but it was in the crofter atmosphere of Stratheden he breathed the manly perseverance and shrewd common-sense he afterwards turned to so good account. And what has been done may be done again. Let a prosperous crofter peasantry be encouraged—towards which many think larger crofts, leases, and instruction in scientific land-cultivation would be very helpful—and many possible workers in the trades and professions of the country will be met with in crofter homes. And though this very reason for perpetuating the system may to some appear to be a sure way of causing the crofter system to fade, in reality it is far from being so. The love of the old home is strong in the crofter heart, as in other hearts; and though some may leave the old place for wider spheres of usefulness, it is all but certain the feeling referred to will secure that some one of the family, or one not far removed in the ties of kindred, will wish to occupy the ancestral home and croft.

CHAPTER II.

RELIGION OF A HIGHLAND PARISH OF TO-DAY.

BY many the religious beliefs and ways prevalent among Highlanders have long been believed to be largely tinged with narrowness if not with fanaticism, and to partake very largely of a *gloomy* hue. The allegation, to some extent, may be true, but it may be misleading. There is, of course, no clear reason why a gloomy religion should prevail in one district of the country more than in another, on account of its geographical situation. No doubt one cannot help thinking that the *remote loneliness* of the mountain-girt habitations of many of the Highlanders may have tended to foster gloomy if not superstitious thoughts. Taking this for granted, the student of the history of religious development will watch with interest the results of the fact that the remoteness indicated is disappearing before steamers, railways, and the telegraph. In connection with such influence as the remoteness may have had, it may be worth considering whether something of the nature of a gloomy superstition may not belong to the religion of all peoples in the primitive or earlier stage of their history. Assuming this to be the case, the remoteness of the Highlands generally—a remoteness which, until recently, had a great influence—would have helped to perpetuate the primitive ways of thinking, and a gloomy aspect would long colour the religious views of the northern Highlanders. A wave of progress, however, aided in its advance by the travelling facilities of to-day, has since spread over the country generally; and though, perhaps, it was longer of reaching the far north, it did come, and its enlightening effects — which, marvellous to relate, some people were slow to welcome—are daily becoming more extended and appreciated.

It would be a pity, however, if it were thought that anything of the nature of a *fatal* error belonged to the prevalent type of religion in Highland parishes of other days. Indeed, to this hour, and with some truth, many are ready to accord the religious Highlander of, say, some forty or fifty years ago, a high place for devoutness and piety.

"The piety of the north," "the devout Highlander," "the serious Celt" are terms in frequent use in some quarters with reference to the period indicated. Nor, perhaps, can better instances of simple-minded piety be found than were some of the native residents of a Highland parish of that time, and suchlike ones as are yet to be met with. Genuinely reverent, they live under the influence of an abiding sense of the nearness of the unseen world, and each step seems made as if in the presence of an all-seeing One. They have their failings, of course, of the head and also of the heart, but the persons referred to are such as one cannot but feel interested in, not only because of their, generally speaking, guileless ways and devout life, but also because they form the diminishing few of a type of character rapidly fading away. Not that the Highland character, religiously or otherwise, is necessarily deteriorating. It would, indeed, evidence a very feeble faith in religion if it could be believed that it must fade before the advance of progress and general enlightenment. So far as the Highland character is concerned, though some of its simpler, and perhaps guileless, aspects may be disappearing, it is generally believed to be growing in breadth, industriousness, and general usefulness. Notwithstanding this, very many look back regretfully upon a past of some forty years ago as the "good old days" in the religious history of the northern Highlanders—and no doubt, in every Highland parish then and for some time after, the type we have referred to was pretty largely represented. Simple faith and hopeful trust were prominent features in the character of those alluded to. They knew or felt little or nothing of the bitter venomous animosity sectarianism is so fertile of; and though certain of their views regarding the Creator may have been crude, if not false, this theoretical weakness was condoned by the simple hopeful way in which they invariably trusted in the Supreme Being. Subsequent to the secession of '43 from the Established Church of Scotland, when the great majority of the northern Highlanders forsook the Church of their fathers, such representatives of the type of character here remarked on as were found in the ranks of the opposing parties were innocent of the uncharitableness and evil-speaking too many on both sides were guilty of.

Into the question between the two Presbyterian bodies composing the religious denominations of the greater number of our Highland parishes we do not choose to enter. Such an inquiry is foreign to our purpose, and is, as a rule, profitless. After all the wrangling of the past, the many unhappy squabblings at, and since, Disruption times—squabblings too well known in Highland parishes—nothing has been made clearer than that in both the Free and the Established Church there are good men and true, as also false men and vile. This fact, though surely obvious enough, many persons of both denominations apparently forget.

Within recent years there are two matters that have occasioned no small noise and anxiety in Highland parishes, as in other places—the so-called "Union" question, and the case of Professor Robertson Smith. The Union negotiations—that is, the steps taken by the Free Church (for the United Presbyterian Church seemed passive in the matter) towards union with the latter Church—suddenly collapsed about ten years ago, after having engaged the attention of the Free Church for many years previously. In the Highlands generally the great majority of the clergy and laity of the Free Church were opposed to the union, and the dislike to entertain the idea is as strong to-day as it ever was. Here and there a solitary instance was met with of a Free Church clergyman in the Highlands being a "unionist." Some of his anti-union brethren, and anti-union members of even his own congregation, often enough made the ground hot for him, though scarcely so hot as the region to which, as we have been credibly informed, certain Free Church people — and clergymen too, we were particularly surprised to hear—were wont in Disruption days to relegate "Moaderats," as the Established Church people were called by the native Free Church people. Although the Union negotiations have broken down, the bitterness of feeling occasioned has not yet disappeared; and very probably it would be as difficult for the great majority of those who were against the union to explain clearly why they were or are so, as it would be for the Free Church leaders in favour of union to explain why they ever initiated the negotiations. The clergy and laity of the Established Church in the Highlands, as a rule, took little interest in the matter, though we have heard several of them allege that one of the objects aimed at by those favourable to union—the main object, indeed—was the overthrow of the Established Church, the endowments of which are believed to be a source of much irritation to the voluntaries of the Free Church. But we must not here discuss the Union question. It only remains for us to add on this subject, that it was generally understood that it was the large and determined opposition to union manifested in Highland parishes that very much led to the sudden and somewhat remarkably manœuvred step that resulted in the collapse of the Union negotiations.

Scarcely had the Union question been shelved when the perplexing Robertson Smith case turned up. This alleged heresy occasioned, and still occasions, much anxiety and alarm in the north generally; and by at least three-fourths of the Free Church population, and by not a few, as well, of the "Moaderats," the young Professor is regarded as a very *dangerous* person. A very prevalent opinion regarding him in Highland parishes is, that he wishes, so say many, "to take bits away from the Bible, and no believe what Moases said." Fully as hearty and prevalent, if not more so, in Highland parishes, was the condemnation of Professor Smith, and his views regarding "bits of the Bible," as was the dislike to the proposed coalition with the United Presbyterian Church; and the judgment of the Free Church Assembly of 1880 in favour of the Professor caused much and deep anxiety among Free Church people generally in Highland parishes, where the decision was as little expected as it was hoped for. The subsequent and much-talked-of action of a section of the Free Church has been cordially welcomed by Free Church Highlanders generally, the eagerly-hoped-for result being that the suspected Professor should be "putten oot o' the Church."

There are two churches in Stratheden—an Established and a Free—and the great majority of the inhabitants adhere to the latter, which is the case in the northern Highlands generally. The adherents of the Established Church, admitting the numerical superiority of the Free Church, are in the habit of insinuating that the more intelligent and influential of the residents of our Highland parishes adhere to the Establishment; and it is amusing, though scarcely creditable to the good sense of either party, to hear how the one side upbraids the other with weakness in intelligence and influence, and how that other retorts with the insinuation about numerical feebleness. Peter Ross, an adherent of the Established Church in Stratheden, in discussing this matter the other day with Alexander Maclean, a neighbour, and an adherent of the Free Church, said: "Ah, man, Sandy, ye hev a lot o' them; but the quaalatty, and the ones that hess eddikayshan, goes to oor Church, the good ould Church o' Scotland." "Och, maybe yuss, Peter," was the reply; "but look in your Bible—*if you'll be reading it;* surely you'll be reading it—and if you wull, you'll see the quaalatty and some o' the big rich chaps 'ull no hev much chance some day, Peter. What does the Bible say aboot the rich ones, and the cawmall and the needle, and going in through the needle? What wull eddikayshan and quaalatty do *then,* Peter?" "Be quate, Sandy; you're worse nor a cawmall yourself," vigorously retorted Peter. "Surely there's no harm in quaalatty and eddikayshan; and surely if they'll be good themselves, that wull no spoil them. P'raps, Sandy, you're only kind o' vexed ye hevna some o' the money and the grandar o' the quaalatty in your own Church. Indeed, the Free Church is ferry foand o' money, and they'll be askin' of people that hessna much to give; and they're ferry soary to pairt wi' it; but they must be like their neeburs, and they'll give it."

In Stratheden almost all the "big fairmers" adhere to the "Auld Kirk," but the great majority of the crofters and natives attend the Free Church. In using the term "natives," it is proper to observe that in Stratheden, as in most other Highland parishes of to-day, there is a considerable number of "strangers." One of the "big fairmers" is a native of one of the south-eastern counties of Scotland, one is an Aberdonian, another hails from the south of England, while a fourth comes from Lanarkshire. Besides these there are ploughmen from Banffshire, shepherds from Roxburgh and Northumberland, and gamekeepers from England and from Aberdeenshire. A very large proportion of this imported element adhere to the Church of Scotland; but it is beyond our province to inquire whether all these are to be included among those indicated by Peter Ross when he referred to "the quaalatty and the people that hess eddikayshan."

There was a time in Stratheden, and in too many Highland parishes, when the feeling between the adherents of the two Churches was, to say the least, not what it ought to have been. Bitter, very bitter, things were said on both sides, but we leave it to those that know the facts, to say on which side the greater bitterness was displayed. Instances —too many—might be given of the venomous and silly things said of and to each other, by the *Christians* of that time; but it would serve no good purpose to repeat them, and far be it from us to say anything that would revive memories of sayings and doings that "good men and true," of whatever Church, would like to forget.

Happily such silly nonsense as is understood to have been prevalent in those days is not now, to any great extent at least, heard. No doubt some rather remarkable statements are even yet put forward. Only a few years ago, as we were informed by a Free Church clergyman, a north-Highland divine of the Free Church, in addressing his congregation, made reference to "the Moderates," and said: "Ah, my friends, there are three kinds of people like each other; and, my friends, these three kinds of people that are like each other are the Pawgans, the *Moderates*, and the Hottentots. And what do you think now, my friends, of the Moderates? Ah! what do you think of them?" This instance of pulpit sectarianism—the pulpit displays more of this unworthy feeling than the pew—is mild compared with what has been heard, and is chronicled partly as an evidence of the absurdities into which feeble narrowness drives some people. Though matters are happily more promising nowadays—traces of the old feeling now and then appear. There was too much of it noticeable at the recent school board elections, and more than enough of it crops up at school board and certain other public meetings.

The people of Stratheden, generally speaking, attend church regularly. In the busier seasons of the year—spring and harvest—the attendance is thinner. Many of the crofters and others are hard wrought, and the distance from church in many cases is great; accordingly they elect to sleep at home in preference to sleeping in church; and this is wise, for the spring and autumn "nap" might be an awkwardly prolonged one.

This may be a suitable place for referring to the matter of Sunday observance in a Highland parish of to-day. Highlanders have long been understood greatly to revere this day, and they have also been credited with encouraging a narrow, and even superstitious, estimate of the right observance of the "Sawbath." As a rule they did and do revere the day, and some of them did observe it narrowly, and perhaps superstitiously, though this latter fact can scarcely be considered peculiar to Highlanders. Narrower views, however, are giving way to more cheerful and healthier ways of thinking, though even yet traces of the old feeling are discernible. Some of the older people in Stratheden, think it not right to laugh or go out to breathe the fresh air on "Sawbath," though they can quite tolerate, and even practise, uncharitable gossip, lying, and scandal in their homes on the sacred day. Some of this class, steeped in the chilling unhealthiness of the letter-and-form sort of religion, will not allow their children to have their honest laugh, or even look at picture-books of the most useful kind, on "Sawbath;" but these same people will afford their children on the same day an opportunity of hearing how they (the parents) can talk enviously and falsely of their neighbours, and, as is sometimes the case, utter language of a kind decidedly unfavourable to the moral training of the young. One of the older natives of a Highland parish of to-day gravely assured us in conversation not long ago, that the people were "growing awful careless and baad" now, because, as he proceeded to observe, "in my younger days you wouldna see any person at all oot on Sawbath, exceptin' the people going to the preachin'. The children wouldna say a word nor laugh, nor go oot o' the door, nor anything, and not a living would go near a well for wattur, and it's hardly some o' the people would wash themselves on Sawbath! But ochan! ochan! that's no the way in the day that's int now. I am seeing young people, yes, and ould people, *walking*, yes, and *jumping* too, on the braes, and the *children* will be oot, and people are fearful dressy and grawnd on the Sawbath." Happily, more enlightened views, generally speaking, prevail in a

Highland parish of to-day. The wave of progress that spread over the country generally has now made itself felt. The educational machinery has been enlarged and improved, while travel has helped to leaven the narrowness and gloom of the northern Highlands with the broader, more cheerful, and healthier views prevalent in more highly favoured centres of intelligence and general progress. There is a large and growing circulation of excellent Sunday literature, and the general result is a clearer appreciation of the truth that "the Sabbath was made for man, and not man for the Sabbath."

In Stratheden Gaelic and English are preached regularly in the Free and Established Churches. Both parsons are well up in the Gaelic language; and this is deserving of notice, because, in some parishes in which Gaelic as well as English is understood to be preached, the Gaelic-speaking attainments of the clergy even are not of a high order. No important interest suffers in consequence, for as a rule, in no Highland parish of to-day is there any but the smallest number that cannot well enough follow all that it is useful to remember of an English sermon; and besides, the defects in Gaelic speaking rarely, if ever, occasion any *pronounced* heresy. At the same time, to those that really know Gaelic, and the proper pronunciation thereof, the blunders of speech thus occurring must sound very ludicrous. We have heard of a case of this kind taking place in a Highland parish, not many years ago, where the preacher in attempting to use the Gaelic equivalents for lost sinners (*peacaich chaillte*) used the words *piocaich shaillte*, these latter words signifying a species of *salted fish* with which the most of the congregation were well acquainted! It will be seen the reverend gentleman was literally *at sea;* and some of our readers can imagine the utter contempt such of the audience as knew Gaelic well would feel for the parson's Gaelic acquirements. The young people, of course, would giggle, while some of the old would sigh. Another equally ludicrous instance of this blundering we had from no other than the reverend gentleman that perpetrated the mistake. He had been alluding to fault-finding in the course of his Gaelic preaching one day, and in quoting the illustration of the beam and the mote, said *an t-saill*, instead of *an t-sail*,—that is, the *fat*, instead of the beam. The difference, to look at both words, does not seem great; but, to those that really know Gaelic, the difference in sound is perceptible enough, and the observation correspondingly grotesque.

In Stratheden, as already said, Gaelic is regularly preached in the Free and Established Churches. Both clergymen are quite at home in the language; and whatever irrelevant or other matter they may utter, there is little danger of either of them perpetrating aught in the style of the ludicrous blunders referred to. In both churches the services of the Sunday begin with the Gaelic portion. In the Established Church the proportion of those that know Gaelic better than English is small; while, in the Free Church, the reverse is understood to be the case. The Gaelic portion of the services occupies more time in the Free Church than in the Established Church,—a practice which satisfies an idea long prevalent among a certain section of Highlanders that sermons are nothing if not long. To this day there are a few in most of our Highland parishes that would view a preacher that would give short sermons as not a *good* man—as being "unsound."

With reference to the relative position of the two languages—Gaelic and English—so far as preaching in Highland churches is concerned, very marked changes have taken place within recent years. Some twenty years ago, in almost all Highland parishes, at the conclusion of the Gaelic services, a considerable number would leave, not being able to understand an English discourse. To-day there are very few parishes, indeed, of which this can be said; and in not a few cases, few, if any, leave until after the English service is over, though some that wait might be found to be by no means accomplished in the English language. Within the last twenty-five years there were some Highland parishes in which there was no English preached, so complete was the sway of Gaelic. The greater number of the better educated portion of the community in those days knew and spoke Gaelic well; while, if there did happen to be any that knew English better than Gaelic, or that knew nothing of the latter, they were favoured with special services. Even to-day, a solitary instance may be met with—especially in the Outer Hebrides—of a church in which English is not *regularly* preached. Last winter we heard an amusing story bearing on this matter from a member of the Free Church. At the time the incident about to be related happened, some three years ago, our informant, an intelligent young lady, had been residing in a district of the Highlands where the Free Church clergyman whose ministrations she usually attended rarely preached English. On a certain Sunday, at the conclusion of the Gaelic service, the reverend gentleman announced that if any present wished to hear an English sermon, he would be glad, on their remaining after the others left, to comply with their request. Our informant and another young lady formed the English congregation for the day. The usual preliminaries over, the preacher proceeded to give a discourse mainly taken up with a violent and rambling tirade against drunkenness, and quarrels of the pugilistic sort! which his fair "audience"—both highly respectable—indignantly felt, and rightly so, to be altogether out of place in the circumstances. To add to the unpleasantness of the situation, the preacher in the course of his remarks, roaring loudly all the while in violent declamatory fashion anent the evils of intemperance, observed, to the amazement, and indeed confusion, of his *congregation*, that, while on a visit to a town in the south, he had himself seen a drunken man careering wildly in the street in a semi-nude state! the reverend declaimer expressing this latter fact in language far from elegant. In ordinary circumstances, of course, the audience would have remained to thank the clergyman for the *special* privilege afforded them, but the reader need hardly be told they were only too glad to get away.

In addition to the Sunday services, there are in most Highland parishes, and chiefly in connection with the Free Church, week-day gatherings going under the name of "prayer-meetings," held fortnightly, and attended by the clergyman, one or more of his elders, and a few others, the audience present being chiefly old women. These prayer-meetings used to be pretty well attended some twenty years ago, but nowadays they seem less popular, and it is difficult to avoid the conclusion that at no distant period they will, as a distinct institution, cease to exist. Some of those that attend these week-day prayer-meetings are simple-minded and really pious people, representing a type of religious character not so numerous now as some fifty years back; but, though the absence of the particular type of character we have referred to near the commencement of this chapter, is becoming more and more marked, the bountiful compensating resources of the Ruler of the universe are providing another type equally good, though after another fashion. Accordingly, though the gatherings alluded to are not attended by a tithe of the numbers that flocked to them in other days, some thirty, and even fifteen, years ago, those that love the Highlands, and pray for their prosperity, need not suspect that such a change necessarily indicates any religious or moral declension among the people.

The religious event of the year, in a Highland parish, is the Communion season, or, as some of the people call it, "the Saycriemant time," which is more of an event, because, except in a very few cases, it takes place once a-year only. To the Communion in the Established Church, which, as in the Free Church, takes place but once a-year in the great majority of places, very few come from other parishes; while of those that are present at the Free Church Communion, large numbers are from neighbouring parishes, not a few coming from places twenty and even forty miles away.

A remarkable feature in the case of the Free Church is the very small number of communicants in proportion not merely to the number of people attending the Communion, but also to the size of each separate congregation. There have been reasons advanced in explanation of this somewhat remarkable phenomenon, but they have been chiefly by interested persons, and are not edifying. In point of fact, the clergy must blame themselves for the paucity of communicants they now and then deplore. They long preached an unattainable ideal of fitness for Communion,—strangely forgetting that the ordinance is a *means* towards piety, and not an *end*. This manner of presenting the matter was long too prevalent in both the Free and Established Churches in Highland parishes, though not peculiar to them, since it was a common idea in very many other districts of the country. For some Sundays previous to the Communion, the clergy were in the habit of explaining the ordinance, and of specifying the qualities necessary for entitling persons to communicate worthily; and too often the effect of these haranguings was to impart an utterly distorted estimate, and to deter some sensitive but piously inclined individuals from making public profession of their faith in, and love to, a self-sacrificing perfect Example. On the Sunday of the Communion, in many cases, the scare was complete. What is called the "fencing of the tables"—telling from the pulpit what persons are and are not worthy communicants—was gone about in so unthinking a fashion as to actually frighten many sensitive souls. To this day this feature holds an unhappy sway. Congregations, accordingly, numbering in each case some five or six hundred people, can with difficulty command fifty communicants; and it is a specially noticeable and disappointing feature, that few, if any, under forty years of age sit at the Communion-table in the Free Church in an average Highland parish. The most of the few that do communicate are aged, the young and the greater number of the middle-aged remaining content with being spectators of the event.

The Communion season in a Highland parish is, in its main features, very much the same as it was thirty and even fifty years ago. The same number of days are occupied, the same order of service is employed, the same remarkable fewness of communicants is noticeable; and though it is understood that the number coming from distant parishes is not now quite so large, there is still a considerable flocking of people from far-away places.

It may be proper to observe that our remarks on this subject have almost exclusive reference to the Communion season in connection with the Free Church. The Communion takes place in the Established Church on the same day; but there are *special* features connected with the services in the Free Church, and the latter denomination being that to which the great majority of the people—and especially the natives—of the greater number of Highland parishes belong, we think it better to speak specially of the Communion season in the Free Church. Before we do so, however, it may be well to mention one or two features special to the Established Church Communion season. Few go from one parish to another to the Communion in the latter Church. The *Friday* services, which we will shortly allude to, are almost unknown in the Established Church, though in a solitary instance what is called "a prayer-meeting" may take place on that day. "You have no Friday," is the rather odd way in which some Free Church people remind adherents of the Established Church of the absence of Friday services in the latter Church. We are not aware whether this *lack-a-day* observation is keenly felt by the "Moaderats." In the Established Church, the number of communicants, relatively to the size of the congregation, is very much larger than is the case in the Free Church. Certain people in the latter denomination have a way of explaining this last phenomenon by insinuating that the ideal of fitness for the ordinance is not so high as it ought to be among the local Established Church authorities, and that the Church discipline generally is not so strict as it should be. It is quite foreign to our purpose to inquire into the truth or otherwise of this allegation. It may be one of those strange comments which persons of different *Christian* denominations are so fond — and fully as much in

Highland parishes as in other places—of making regarding each other. Of course no intelligent unprejudiced observer of the community generally in a Highland parish, or any other parish, we suppose, will believe that there is any marked difference, religious or moral, between the adherents of the one Church and those of the other.

The Communion season begins on Thursday, and extends over five days, closing on Monday. A considerable number of strangers arrive in the place of meeting on Wednesday night; and we have heard it said, that so busy are some of the residents providing for the wants of their friends and acquaintance from a distance, that not a few of the former are prevented from attending the services. Thursday, the Fast-day, on the whole, is pretty strictly observed in most Highland parishes of to-day. A change, however, seems coming. The holiday practice, now so common in other places on the so-called Fast-day, is beginning to be adopted in the Highlands generally, and promises not long hence to be the order of the day.

Friday, strange to say, continues to be considered by many the most enjoyable day of the Communion season. Whereas on the Thursday, in many cases, the church can accommodate the worshippers, the

Friday services almost invariably take place in the open air, and on this day those called "the Men" have the field very much to themselves. They do the greater part of the speaking, and Friday is popularly known as "the Men's" day. These persons, known in the Free Church only, are a class of people believed to be more or less eminent for piety, well versed in the Scriptures, and somewhat endowed with the speaking gift. On Friday a portion of Scripture is selected for remark, on which ordinarily about eight or nine of the Men make comments, with, as a rule, special reference to what are termed the marks or evidences of the Christian character, and more or less lengthened observations on the believer's *experiences* generally. During the time the Men are talking, the ministers—of whom as many as half-a-dozen are frequently assembled on these occasions—are sitting in the "tent" or wooden box which constitutes the open-air pulpit for the time being. One of the clergymen present is supposed to preside on the Friday, opening the proceedings, and, after the Men have said their say, summing up, so to speak, the varied comments made, and closing the proceedings; but to all intents and purposes Friday is exclusively set apart to give the Men an opportunity of holding forth,—the term "the Men" being employed to distinguish them from the ministers, or usual speakers.

The Men have frequently been spoken of in some quarters sneeringly, in terms that would lead one to believe they are a spiritually proud, self-sufficient, fanatical, ignorant, and indeed hypocritical class of persons. It would be utterly unfair to apply all or any of these terms to them as a class. As in every other class of human beings, there will be found among them some that display one or other, or even more than one, of the uninviting features specified; but such sweeping denunciation of the Men as we have sometimes heard, is open to the suspicion of a prejudice against the Men themselves or the Church to which they belong. At the same time we can as little understand why, as a class, they should be considered pre-eminently good, as why they should be referred to in terms of sneering suspicion. There are among them, no doubt, persons of a type of character not more prevalent than could be wished,—simple-minded Christians, most eager to do what they believe to be right, and more diligent in watching themselves than in trying to detect faults in their neighbours. But among the Men there are also individuals with heart and soul very little, if at all, leavened by the

Gospel of light and love, and wofully void of the large-heartedness of the Christianity they profess and *talk* so much about. Among them likewise may be found unthinking disciples of an unhealthy mysticism—persons too prone to lose sight of Gospel morality in a superstitious, if not Pharisaic, desire to be reckoned models of what they consider religious orthodoxy. Some of them are self-sufficient, though it is proper to remember that the popularity they enjoy constitutes a strong temptation to this sort of weakness. Some of them are ignorant enough—but of course this cannot be said to be always a crime. Some of them are hypocritical—but, unfortunately, this fault cannot be considered peculiar to the Men. A few of them entertain rather uninviting views regarding the Supreme Being—but it can hardly be believed that in this respect the Men will be found to be alone. In short, they are *men* as well as *the* Men, with the ordinary characteristics of frail humanity, and, undoubtedly, to be judged of just like other people.

In the course of their Friday speaking, many of the Men make considerable efforts after saying *smart* things, and many of the audience greatly relish a peculiarity now and then indulged in by some of the Men,—that, namely, of criticising the clergy, or, in a sort of humorously bantering way, assuming the office of monitors to their clerical superiors.

In the days when the contemptible sectarianism so long prevalent in Highland parishes was at its height, these Men were in the habit of saying very extraordinary things about the "Moaderats." Had the destiny of the latter been in the hands of some of the Men, it is very awful to contemplate to what sort of region the "Moaderats" generally would be consigned.

Many Free Church people—some regretfully, but quite as many with indifference—say that the institution of the Men shows unmistakable signs of breaking up; nor, indeed, is it easy to avoid the conclusion that, as a distinctive class, they will not long hence be unknown. Most—all, indeed—of the Men of to-day are aged, and it does not appear that, among the younger section of the Free Church community, anything like a sufficient number of probable aspirants exists to fill their places; nor will the impartial observer see reason to believe that any important interest will suffer from the blank.

Of the Saturday services there is nothing special to say. Then comes the Communion Sunday, or *Sabbath*, as most Highlanders prefer to call it. The services usually begin about an hour before mid-day, and, for fully two hours up till that time, the roads and footpaths leading to the place of concourse are largely peopled by pedestrians, while vehicles of various sorts likewise do duty for the occasion. Many of the worshippers come a great distance, some from places forty miles away; and though some of those present on Sunday have been staying in the place during the other days, the great majority of the Sunday audience are people that come from their homes on the Sunday morning and return the same day. Many are seated long before the services begin. The place of meeting is usually on a slope or brae, at the foot of which stands the "tent" for the preacher. Though it is alleged that in the Highlands generally there is something like a falling off in the number attending these gatherings, the attendance in several instances is yet considerable, and more especially, of course, where there is the attraction of a popular preacher. The services begin in Gaelic—the English service takes place in the church—with the singing of a few verses of a psalm to the tune of Martyrdom or Coleshill, or some such like air; and it is very pleasant to hear the quaint old music rising from the crowd, and gladdening the stillness of the surrounding solitudes. Generally speaking, the aspect of the crowd is devout, and, though it might be rash to take this as evidence of devoutness, there are many bent heads, communicants, especially, seeming cast down, if not gloomy. Among the young people of both sexes there are some not particularly devout-looking. Their attention seems more taken up with themselves and with each other than with the preacher and the occasion of the gathering; and some, old as well as young, show a restlessness, if not a levity, unfitting the solemnity becoming the event. But there are devout worshippers in the crowd, — some that have come at the bidding of a humble but earnest longing to hear the grand old story of the Gospel news, and to take part in a service they view with feelings of genuine humility and veneration.

The Sunday services usually occupy about six hours, the *action* sermon, as it is called, and the "fencing of the tables" taking up a large portion of this time; and, after Communion, there is a concluding address, usually of considerable length. At the conclusion of the Monday services, which do not call for special notice, small groups of people may be seen here and there, some probably commenting on what this or that preacher said, others gossiping on quite other matters, while many who make the

Communion season the occasion of meeting relatives and friends, are wishing each other good-bye.

We have now referred to the more important features of the Communion season in a Highland parish of to-day. There are various reflections suggested by the event, such as the small number of communicants, and the danger of taking the large number assembled as an evidence of the prevalence of an earnest religious life; but into these and kindred questions the purpose of this book does not require us minutely to enter.

We might say a great deal regarding the theological opinions long prevalent in the far north, but we think the reader may gather from what has already been said what the general character of such opinions is, and how the less inviting of them are beginning to give way to brighter and more genial views. Some persons, imperfectly acquainted with the actual circumstances of the Highlands, entertain a wrong estimate of the religious state of these districts. As already indicated, we have long been accustomed to hear of the narrowness, self-righteousness, and bigotry of the Highlands; but while all these features might be met with up till within the last fifteen years even, in sad abundance, and to this day unhappily may be found in some quarters, the fact cannot be said to be peculiar to the Highlands. Besides, so far especially as the bigotry is concerned, justice to the Highland people requires us to bear in mind that, where the bigotry did, and to any extent yet does exist, the spiritual guides of the bigoted ones are principally to blame for this unhealthy feature.

We might easily furnish the reader with highly discreditable proofs of the reign of bigotry and Pharisaism in the Highlands, and as easily might it be shown by what section of the people such bigotry was or is most generally shown, but this would serve no good purpose. We prefer to chronicle the fact that such bigotry is dying out, or, at least, that the growth of enlightened public opinion keeps it in check. By way of antidote to the regret one feels on viewing certain aspects of the ecclesiastical situation in the Highlands, during the period especially from fifteen to thirty years ago, it is pleasing to be able to know that in that period, as to-day, there were Highlanders unchilled by the blight of self-righteous bigotry. These latter (it is not worth asking whether they were Established Church or Free Church adherents) untroubled by questions regarding inspiration, technically so called, lived under the daily inspiration of a sense of duty to

God and man. They did not, like silly fanatics, that even to-day may be met with, think there was no room on the path to a happy hereafter for any but those of their own *denomination*. With all the boasted progress of to-day, no better wish for the prosperity of religion in the Highlands can be cherished than that the simple-minded, generous, humble, and tolerant spirit that characterised the persons referred to, might have a wider and a growing sway in Highland parishes of to-day.

CHAPTER III.

THE POLITICS OF A HIGHLAND PARISH OF TO-DAY.

POLITICS rarely disturb the dream of the average native resident of a Highland parish. The subject is spoken of now and then by the people generally, but very often this is more because of the wish to be considered capable of appreciating "what the papers are saying," than from any clear or earnest interest in the goings on in the political world.

"Men, not measures," is practically the political maxim of such as affect any interest in the matter. As with many others, the man, Whig or Tory, whose name is associated with cheapening tea, sugar, or tobacco, or with reducing the dog-tax, is the favourite politician.

The meaning of even the most rudimentary terms in the political vocabulary would appear to be by some Highlanders rather imperfectly understood.

An old woman in a Highland parish not very far from Stratheden, it is said, once expressed her astonishment at the very great age apparently reached by "that man Goavurmant" (Government). Not only had she heard a great deal about his doings in *her* early days, but her father used to tell her about the same aged "personage" as being spoken of as far back as even *he* could remember. There is a still more remarkable instance of political ignorance which has been related to us as occurring in a Highland parish not fifty miles from Stratheden. A few years ago the then Chancellor of the Exchequer—a peaceably-inclined man, it is necessary to add, in view of what follows—was on a visit to the proprietor of the place, a nobleman famous for his generous and splendid hospitality. On a certain evening during the stay of the Chancellor of the Exchequer at this nobleman's Highland home, a meeting of some kind or other took place in the district, at which, among others, there was present Peter Macgregor, a decent old man, and an elder in one of the churches. At the close of the meeting, and in the ordinary course of conversation, some one happened to mention in Peter's hearing that the Chancellor of the Exchequer was at Dunedin Castle; whereupon the elder, unlettered in the nomenclature of party or office, to the amusement of all that heard him, said,—"Och, dear me! oor own proprietor, he's a goot laird and a goot kind man, but, mercy me! he's an awful man, for there's no a wild beast that's in't but he wull get one of them!" Poor Peter evidently imagined the visitor at the Castle was another trophy of adventurous travel in foreign wilds.

These, of course, are exceptional instances; but so far as the average native resident of a Highland parish of to-day is concerned,—while the *age* of a Government is pretty generally known, and while the mention of the Chancellor of the Exchequer's name does not bring up wild suggestions of a menagerie,—of clear appreciation of party distinctions, or of the significance of the changes in the political atmosphere, there is very little indeed.

So far, however, as can be gathered from such declarations as are ventured upon, so-called Liberal leanings are observable among the younger crofters, farm-servants, and working class generally in Stratheden; while among others the "old way," or as some call it, the "way long ago," understood to signify Conservatism, is rigidly adhered to.

The news of the dissolution of 1880 afforded a special opportunity for ascertaining the political leanings of at least one native resident. A day or two after the news came, we met Angus Sutherland, one of the native residents, a man of fifty years of age and a person of some intelligence, but, as the sequel will show, not specially learned in matters political. "Is this Baykansfield to be putten oot?" was the question put to us by Angus, in order to know what was doing—a question followed, however, by the statement, before we had time to make any observation, "I don't know myself who's best to be in; it's no for the likes o' me to be speaking aboot them things,—it's scholars and people o' that kind it belongs till better to be speaking aboot them things." Being little inclined for a political discussion, we merely made the observation that a few days would tell who would be "oot" or in. At this stage, however, such political leanings as Angus had were beginning to appear, and we began to suspect that, after the manner of some people found in Lowland and Highland parishes of to-day and other days, Angus was assuming ignorance merely in order to hear what we had to say. "Am feared," observed Angus, "this Baykansfield is ower fond o' war—and it's an awful thing war—and forbye the praisheous lives that are lost, it runs away wi' an awful sicht o' money; and now them papers are saying—I reads my newspaper of coorse—that it was an awful baad thing o' Baykansfield to be going to fight them *Soloo* chaps; he should have letten the black lads alone. Now, Maister Mackenzie, won't you say yourself that was no richt? but I don't know myself indeed very weel,—the likes o' me canna oonderstan' them things at all." It will be seen from this last observation that Angus was lapsing into his *sounding* ways, and indeed he seemed most anxious to know what manner of person we were politically. "Well, Angus," we replied, "war is always a sad business; and, no doubt, rightly or wrongly, a great many persons are of opinion that the Government of Lord Beaconsfield might have prevented some of those wars in which our country has been recently engaged abroad; and you may depend upon it, Angus, all that think so will do their utmost to send Lord Beaconsfield and his party to the right-about." "Weel, sir," was the reply of Angus, "that's what I was thinking myself, although, as I was telling ye, the likes o' me doesna oonderstan' just much aboot them things; but I put no doot you'll know all aboot it; but, Maister Mackenzie, is there a *pairty* wi' Baykansfield? I thocht there was none but himself for them wars, and that this Gladstone was the other way, just complete contrary like to Baykansfield." A little elucidation now obviously became necessary, and we resolved to attempt the matter, although the very rudimentary political education seemingly possessed by Angus was slightly discouraging. "You must understand, Angus," we proceeded to observe, necessarily using the simplest possible style of explanation, "Beaconsfield could do nothing unless there was a large number of the members of Parliament of the same opinion as himself, and helping him to carry out his plans. The British Parliament is made up of two kinds of persons; they call the one party Liberals, and the other party Conservatives." "Am a Reebural," exclaimed Angus; "am that indeed, sir, because the paper is saying—I reads my newspaper, of coorse—that the Reeburals, not the other chaps, is the richt sort o' fellows, and that they'll give the poor man, and every other body, everything they'll be wanting. Och, yes, Maister Mackenzie, am a Reebural, although the likes o' me doesna know much aboot it; but Gladstone's my man; he's the man for me." "Very well, Angus," we replied, "you're quite right to have your own opinion in the matter; but wait a little," we added, "till I explain matters further. The chief man in the Government is called the Premier, or Prime Minister." "Och, dear me!" interposed Angus, with an air of anxious astonishment; "I didna know that *munnistarrs* was in Parliament at all. My word, these munnistarrs, you'll find them looking aifter all kinds o' high places and the likes o' that. They should stop at hoam and be more humbler and give longer sermons. Och, the munnistarrs are no what they were in my younger days, Maister Mackenzie; am feared they're getting ower prood and high kind, and they're crabbed kind and *that*, if you'll no please them and give plenty money at the collekshans." "Dear me, Angus," we replied, "what is all this for? the Prime Minister or Minister of the Crown is not the same as a preaching minister or church minister. The real meaning of minister is a servant, and, speaking of the Government, the term "prime minister" means that the person so named is the chief servant of the Crown or of the Queen. But, Angus, I am quite surprised to hear how you speak about ministers. Of course they have their faults, and some of them are proud enough, and some greedy enough; but you speak very strongly, almost bitterly, against them. I always thought you had a great regard for the clergy, and that you were a very regular attendant at church." "Ah, well," replied Angus,

"I attends church,—that's my duty, Maister Mackenzie; but matters aboot churches are no what they were in my younger days; but oor own munnistarr, Maister Nicolson (Angus adhered to the Free Church), am thinking is a quate man, and preaches longer nor some o' them, and I must say this for him forbye, that he's awful against that fearful fellow—is he Robert Smuss, or Robertson, or Smuss, or what is he?—the fearful fellow that they're saying wants Deuturranoamy putten oot o' the Bible; and that's a grand quaality in oor munnistarr. But, och, I shouldna be speaking aboot munnistarrs. I used to hear my daesant ould faither saying it wasna canny to be speaking aboot munnistarrs, and the likes o' me doesna know much aboot it."

At this stage of our interview with Angus Sutherland we had reached the Stratheden post-office, near which, as is usual on the arrival of the evening mail-train from the south, there was a considerable number of persons—including some half-dozen ploughmen, as many crofters, seven or eight tradesmen (tailors, shoemakers, and joiners), one or two individuals of no occupation, and half a score of boys. This varied assemblage, of course, arranged themselves into small groups for purposes of gossip. But—and this bears out the remarks made at the commencement of this chapter—although it was now some days after the announcement of the dissolution of Parliament had been known in Stratheden, the political situation was very little, if at all, referred to by these people. There were, however, two men at the post-office of Stratheden that evening who affected some interest in the elections, and seemed eager to speak about the matter. One of these was Angus McLeod, a Stratheden crofter, a consequential and somewhat opinionative individual; and the other was George Mackay, a mason in Stratheden, a less dogmatic person, and not so well up in politics as Angus McLeod—a fact which, notwithstanding the readiness displayed by the latter, placed George Mackay's political knowledge at a decidedly low ebb. Angus considers himself a Liberal, but George Mackay is not pronounced either way. "Weel, Maister Mackenzie," observed Angus McLeod, "George and me here was speaking aboot them speeches in the papers them days — whatna tormendous long speeches they're puttin' oot just now — them two chaps Gladstan and Dissurally: but that's no Dissurally's name now—he's gotten a new name—it's Bickensfield, is it no, Maister Mackenzie? Myself is a strong Leeberral, — am that indeed ; am terrable for that fine chap Gladstan;

am no for interfering with them Solloo fellows at all, at all. It would be better to give the money to help the poor man than send it for fighting them black ones." Having complimented Angus on his eloquence, we were going to offer a brief observation of a general kind on the question of the hour, when Angus, fond of hearing himself speak, and evidently proud of what he considered his own superior knowledge, went on,—" I canna make oot whatna side my freend George here is on, Maister Mackenzie." George, who, at the time in question, had been working at his trade at Woodfield, the residence of General Howard, put in the rather remarkable observation, " I'm no thinking them *civeelans* will keep the Parlimant very richt at all. I was hearing the General speaking aboot them—he's a fine scholar the General, forbye being a kind man—and he was saying them *civeelans* doesna just know the ways of matters very weel at all, at all!" It will be seen George's political education was decidedly neglected. General Howard, in commenting on the political situation in the hearing of George, would, very probably, have made some allusion to civilians, in contradistinction to persons of his own profession; and George, thinking it right any time and all times to quote the General, uttered the word "civeelans" as mentioned. Angus McLeod seemed utterly confounded by this specimen of political nomenclature advanced by George. Whatever else he might be ignorant of, Angus knew the party names, and evidently felt proud at his own superior information side by side with George Mackay's vague observation about "civeelans." "Gladstan's my man," exclaimed Angus; "Bickensfield is raither foand o' war, and that's no the way to spend the money the poor man should get. We wull soon hev chape tobawca; and I was saying to the wife she would get a cup o' the tea for almost nothing very soon, for Gladstan was to be in."

The "big fairmers" of Stratheden, with one or two exceptions, appear to hold pronounced Liberal opinions, and Mr Malcolm Macgregor, the "big fairmer" at Burnside, happening to be an elector in a neighbouring county where there was a contested election in 1880, travelled some hundred miles to record his vote for the Liberal candidate. Mr Gabriel Langton, Meadowbank, another of the "big fairmers" of Stratheden, though at one time believed to hold decidedly pronounced Conservative opinions, changed his political creed some time or other during the agricultural depression that fell so heavily on most of the farmers within the last four or five years.

Mr Langton suffered severely from this depression, and, somehow or other, he came to associate the Government of the period, the Beaconsfield Ministry, with the hardships of the time, his indignation at the Conservative Ministry reaching a crisis during the sadly prolonged and severe snowstorm of the winter of 1878-79. Notwithstanding that Mr Gabriel Langton's normal style of speech is kindly, and innocent of all bitterness, he, several times in the course of the winter referred to, was heard to utter very strong denunciations of the party in power at the time.

One evening in April 1880, when the election excitement was at its height, the Rev. Mr Cameron, parish minister of Stratheden, Mr Malcolm Macgregor, Mr Langton, and one or two others, including ourselves, happened to meet, and naturally the political doings of the hour soon became the subject of conversation. Mr Langton, who, somehow, thinks he makes an exceedingly clever hit if he says anything of a *teasing* nature regarding the clergy, observed, at an early stage of the conversation, "The parsons"—Mr Langton is very fond of the word "parson"—"winna like the turn the tide has taken. Dizzy (Mr Langton liked to say "Dizzy") is getting a most terrible drubbing with these elections, and let the old fellow take it. It's awful like to think of the way matters went back while he was in office, and *the winter before last crowned everything.*" Mr Cameron seemed more amused than anything else at Mr Langton's way of putting the matter, and particularly at his appearing to address him specially. The clergy of the Established Church of Scotland have long been popularly understood to be Conservatives, and it was on this assumption that Mr Langton made special reference to the "parsons." We may mention, in passing, that the great majority of the Highland clergy—Free and Established—are understood to be Conservative in politics. So far as the parish minister of Stratheden's political sentiments can be ascertained, he is what is ordinarily termed a Liberal-Conservative, and seems to take very good-naturedly the remonstrances of some of his acquaintance—Liberals and Conservatives alike—who persist in advising him to adopt what they call a more decided tone; but the reverend gentleman, whether from stubbornness or indifference, or from an unalterable faith in the soundness of this sort of middle path, smiles at the earnest remonstrances addressed to him by partisans of either side of politics, and, up to this moment, so far as we can learn, he is a Liberal-Conservative. After Mr Langton's reference to the "parsons'" supposed dislike to the turn the tide had taken in the political world, Mr Cameron indicated a wish that Mr Langton should explain why he thought the parsons would not relish the altered situation. "Och, you're a' Conservatives, and you're afraid o' your Kirk," was the reply; whereupon Mr Malcolm Macgregor, a stanch Liberal, and an equally stanch member of the Established Church of Scotland, observed, — "There's no fear of the Church; there's no person worth mentioning seeking to touch the Church at this moment." Mr Macgregor takes what many will be inclined to think a thoroughly sensible and practical view of the Church question. He deprecates mixing up the matter with politics so-called, alleging that there are many decided Liberals — and he instances himself with some pride and enthusiasm — strong supporters of the Established Church of Scotland. "It's *the people*," Mr Macgregor added, "that will decide the Church question when it comes up; and if the majority of the people of Scotland demand disestablishment—which I don't think will be the case in a hurry—whatever Government there is, they must agree to the people's wishes. Let the Church continue to do good useful work, and she's sure to stand many a long day." "I think, Mr Langton," observed the Rev. Mr Cameron, "Mr Macgregor has put the matter in a very sensible light, and besides heartily endorsing our friend of Burnside's views on this matter, I think it unwise of such as are friends of the Church of Scotland to speak and act as if the existence of the Church depended on the support of any political party. Let the ministers and people of the Established Church, by doing and *giving*"—the reverend gentleman emphasised the *giving*, with a significant look all round—"help to make the Church of Scotland a continually increasing power for good, and the friends of the Church need not trouble themselves about disestablishment." Whether it was that Mr Langton thought his reverence was proceeding to sermonise on the subject, or whether it was that he was afraid it was not well enough known that he had become a Liberal some time during the snowstorm of '78-79, Mr Langton abruptly observed—"But you're all afraid Gladstone will be at your Kirk, and pull it down." At this stage Duncan Kennedy, a Stratheden "small fairmer," an adherent of the Free Church, and a somewhat intelligent man, who had been listening attentively to the discussion, seemed desirous of stating his views on the matter. "Am thinkin' mysel'," observed Duncan, "that the munnistarr is perfectly richt aboot this dussisstawblishment; and forbye that, I waas very gled to hear Maister Macgregor speaking the way he did. The dussisstawblishment wunna be in oor day. Am no o' the Estawblish Church mysel', but I wud be very sorry to see the day—I hope I wunna, and I wunna see the day—the good ould Church of oor fathers will be putten doon: I don't think mysel' there's mony wants it putten doon. Look among the people o' this paireesh itsel',—all the Free Church people in it, am sure, would be doonricht against puttin' doon the Estawblish Church; and it's the same in other paireeshes, am sure. Ah! we wunna pairt wi' the Church o' Scotland though we doesna go to it; we goes to the Church we were brocht up in,—am thinking that's the way wi' all of us." Duncan's observations being, by universal consent, accepted as the close of the comments on the Church question, Mr Angus Ferguson, Braeside, a farmer in the parish, proceeded to offer a few comments. Some one had told him farmers were soon to have better times—it might have been Mr Langton, who expected a great deal from the return of the Liberals to power. "I wunder," observed the tenant of Braeside, "what will Glawdstane and them chaps do for us people

F

that's dependin' on the lawnd, and so awful hadden doon them times." (Angus had been long away from Stratheden, and acquired a peculiar accent.) "Ye see, wi' a' their talk and poaleetics and Goavurrments, they canna bring doon oor rents ae bawbee; and forbye, am no shair they can haud thae Amarrican fellaes frae sending sic tremendous cargoes o' meat and a' kinds o' stuff to oor country—and it's they Amarrican lads that's keeping a' things doon i' the price. Am feared nae Goavurrment can mend that, freends." Mr Gabriel Langton, a convert of depression times to Liberalism, as the reader will remember, scarcely seemed to relish Mr Angus Ferguson's blunt way of putting matters, and, in reply to Ferguson's observations, said: "Wait, Angus, and you'll see all things getting into right order when Gladstone and his party get into power, though it's not just an awfully easy business to put right what Dizzy (Gabriel *would* call him Dizzy) put wrong."

Just as the conference was breaking up, Hugh Fraser, an aged native, understood by a certain class to be a "*good*" man, happened to be passing, and, having asked one of those present what the subject of conversation had been, was supplied with a brief summary of the discussion. "Am no going to say anything aboot Goavurrmants," observed Hugh; "but perhaps if the big fairmers wouldna be setting their hairts on the big sheep and the cattle and the land, they would get better weather, am thinkin'; and they needna be speakin' aboot price —they're gettin' price enough already—that's what they are. Waas the Moaderat munnistarr" (Hugh adhered to the Free Church) "speakin' aboot big sheep and prices? Och, indeed I needna ask that —am sure he was; for they're fairmers, plenty of them Moaderat munnistarrs wi' their glebes, and some o' them hessna much more to do." (This last observation was meant as a sneer at the fewness of adherents of the Established Church in some Highland parishes.) "Ochan, ochan! it's the day that's int that's no easy to be thinkin' of when munnistarrs will be speakin' aboot big sheep and prices with the big fairmers." No one seemed inclined to interrupt Hugh Fraser in his silly harangue. The reader may be curious to know why Fraser passed as a "good" man, seeing he could utter such unmitigated sillinesses as were embodied in his comments on the conference. A perusal of the second chapter of this book may enable the reader to solve the problem. Happily, however, persons of Hugh's way of thinking are becoming a small and rapidly diminishing class. He wound up his rambling comments by saying, "But I needna wunder aboot Moaderat munnistarrs. With my two eyes I saw one o' them walkin' aboot his glebe on *Saiturday*, and lookin' at the cattle and the fields and the gress —fine preparaishan for Sawbath!"

CHAPTER IV.

LANGUAGE AND LITERATURE IN A HIGHLAND PARISH OF TO-DAY.

LOOKING at the matter from the sentimental side—influenced, that is to say, by our affection for the language, founded on fond associations and memories of the days of yore—we were glad to see it stated recently that to-day even, in Scotland, there are three hundred thousand people that speak Gaelic; though, to those that know anything of the Highlands of to-day, it did not require the newspaper correspondence this announcement called forth to explain that it would be absurd to add the little word "only" to the words "that speak Gaelic" in the foregoing sentence. At this moment there are in Scotland something like one hundred and seventy what may be called Highland parishes — places where Gaelic used to be largely spoken and regularly preached, and representing about two hundred and fifty thousand of a population; but, taking Stratheden as an instance—and it is fairly representative—the most enthusiastic admirer of Gaelic would find it difficult indeed, in all these parishes, to discover one hundred and twenty-five thousand —that is, one-half of the aggregate population— that *habitually* use the Gaelic language. There may be instances in which the proportion of Gaelic-speaking ones—those speaking it habitually, we mean—is larger, but there are at least as many where it is smaller; and, taking a public school in the average Highland parish of to-day, and hearing the children talking on the playground, it will be found that English is the prevailing language; nor would it be easy, in the case of some Highland schools, with, say, sixty scholars, to find twenty, or one-third, able to speak Gaelic. This latter fact is suggestive enough, and indicates more clearly than many will care to think, how surely, if slowly, Gaelic as a spoken language is disappearing. All honour, all the same, to Professor Blackie—a good man and true—for his laborious and persevering efforts to preserve the Gaelic language by establishing a Celtic Chair. Every true Highlander must appreciate with a sort of affectionate respect the learned and witty Professor's endeavours in this direction. But, with all his enthusiasm, he is too wise to aim at preserving Gaelic as a *spoken* language. Professor Blackie has no such dream in his mind's eye. The S.G.C.C. (Solicitor-General for the Celtic Chair), as we think he called himself at one time, and C.G.S.I. (Chief of the Gaelic Society of Inverness), which position, and very deservedly, he occupied not long ago, is no visionary. In his witty, brilliant way, he is a far-seeing discerner of the signs of the times, and knows as well as any, and, doubtless, regrets as fondly as most, that while the Gaelic language, for philological and historical purposes generally, deserves to be preserved, the days of Gaelic-speaking must not very long hence cease to be. All honour, likewise, to the Gaelic Society of Inverness, 'The Celtic Magazine,' 'The Gael,' and 'The Highlander,' for their efforts in the same direction. And there are others whom the admirers of the Gaelic language will think of with grateful recollections,—the "bard" of the Gaelic Society of Inverness (Mary M'Kellar, an ardent and clever supporter of Gaelic); Sheriff Nicolson of Kirkcudbright, an eloquent writer, in prose and verse, on Celtic themes; the Rev. Dr Clerk, parish minister of Kilmalie, an accomplished Gaelic scholar; the Rev. Dr M'Lauchlan, Free Church minister, Edinburgh, a very able

Gaelic scholar, and an eloquent writer on Celtic themes generally. There are others that might be mentioned equally enthusiastic in matters affecting the welfare of the Highland people and the Gaelic language, but here we must rest content with enumerating a few of those that take a more prominent part. The matter of Gaelic-speaking has recently been receiving no small attention, on account of the remarkably successful efforts, already referred to, towards founding a Celtic Chair in Scotland, and partly on account of efforts—not, however, quite so successful, though equally enthusiastic—for encouraging the teaching of Gaelic in Highland schools.

The Celtic Chair proposal somewhat perplexed some of the less learned in Stratheden and other Highland parishes—the use of the word "chair" causing especial wonderment. At the time the Chair agitation was at its height, the matter was discussed one evening in one of the Stratheden shops. "What is that Chair they're speakin' aboot just now for the Gaelic?" observed Hugh Mackay, a person of over fifty years of age, and one of the few in the parish that speak Gaelic oftener than English. "What hess a chair to do with our good language?" "Perhaps," replied Donald Morison, another of the party, "it's a praesant o' a chair they're going to give to that cluvvur great scholar Professor Blackie, because he's awful good at keeping up the Gaelic." "Nonsense!" exclaimed the shopkeeper, who had been reading about the matter; "the Gaelic Chair" (the wider designation Celtic is not in common use) "means that there's to be a professor to be teaching Gaelic, like the way they'll be teaching the Greek and the Layteen." "Oh, well, well," observed Donald Morison, "am no wundering at that at all, because it's a grawnd language the Gaelic, and oor forefathers waas speaking it, and every person should learn it. I hope they'll get a man that's very good at the Gaelic to make the scholars learn it smairt and right." "Who's to be making the scholars learn the Gaelic?" inquired George Macrae,—in common with some others present, rather at sea on the Chair question: "they couldna do better nor take old Sandy Macgillivray at Cnoc-abartach, and put him in a chair, and they'll get plenty Gaelic, and very good Gaelic, and the best Gaelic, am sure. I think that myself whatevvur." "All very well," observed David Macdonald, an intelligent crofter in the parish, "but the Gaelic is going out of fashion; indeed I think it is going to die out altogether. It doesna pay, and that's the long and short of it. People doesna need it for places and situations and the like o' that, although it's a good fine language, and many excellent people before us had no language but the Gaelic." These latter observations of Macdonald rather displeased another crofter present, who was somewhat of an enthusiast on the side of Gaelic. "What hairum, am sure," said Hugh Maclean, the enthusiast alluded to, "can the Gaelic do for situations and places? Many's the good, cluvvur man in splendid situations that hess plenty Gaelic, and it's no hairum to him." Macdonald was not wishful to prolong the discussion, and this was well. Like many others discussing the same theme, the one viewed the matter from a sentimental point of view, and the other from a utilitarian standpoint, which, of course, rendered agreement very improbable, if not impossible.

Some thirty years ago all the inhabitants of our Highland parishes, with very few exceptions, could speak Gaelic. School-children could then whisper to each other across the school-benches in that language; and they spoke it, and it chiefly, on the playground, a fact that never seemed seriously to interfere with the progress of their English education. At the time indicated, Gaelic was spoken, as often, at least, as English, in most Highland homes, while in some families it was the language exclusively used. It was preached in all Highland churches, and in not a few it alone was preached. All this is now changed. Except in certain districts of the Outer Hebrides, with solitudes unbroken by the whistle of a railway train, few school-children in a Highland parish of to-day whisper Gaelic across the school-benches, or utter it loudly on the playground. In some parishes where, twenty years ago, three hundred persons might be found able to speak Gaelic *only*, it will to-day be difficult to find twenty unable to speak English. But the most significant feature of the changed days of Gaelic is its growing disuse among the rising generation—a fact already alluded to. Nor is it void of significance that some of the older people that yet use Gaelic find it necessary occasionally to interpolate an English word, and that in some districts of the Highlands not a few people to-day speak a Gaelic largely mixed with English words, although, for the English words so used, any one desiring to know Gaelic might easily find a Gaelic equivalent.

Gaelic prospects in Stratheden share the altered fortunes of the language. Some, no doubt, among the older natives speak Gaelic habitually, rarely speaking English—though most of them can speak it—but these form a rapidly diminishing number. There are some in the parish—one or two of the "big fairmers," a shepherd or two, a gamekeeper, and a gardener—that have no Gaelic; and this, in its way, is an accession to the wave that goes to sweep away the language as a spoken tongue. With these exceptions, most of the inhabitants know Gaelic, but they also know English, and their children in the greater number of instances know the latter language better and speak it oftener; nor should it be forgot, as being especially significant in regard to this matter, that in many Highland parishes of to-day there are not a few of the rising generation ignorant of Gaelic.

The English spoken by the average native resident in a Highland parish of to-day is scarcely of the kind some would wish us to believe. In the miscellaneous columns of some provincial newspapers, and in a few publications far more ambitious, there are now and then specimens of English, as spoken in the Highlands, ordinarily unknown to actual fact. Those that supply such specimens seem to think it right to speak of *nossing* for nothing, *goot* for good, and like metamorphoses of look and sound, as if it was the English ordinarily spoken in these districts; but such style of pronunciation in the average Highland parish is to-day rare. Not that the English spoken in Highland parishes is always void of Gaelic flavour, but the number of those in the average Highland parish of to-day that for nothing give *nossing*, that avoid good and bad alike, electing to say *goot* and *paad*, is comparatively small, and undoubtedly diminishing. The school, the railway, and the newspaper, are causing these and like peculiarities of pronunciation to disappear; and if, which we are inclined to doubt, in any Highland parish to-day these peculiarities have anything like a marked existence, it must be because such parish is not, or has not long been, sharing the improving influences of the agencies specified.

And now for the kind of *literature* usually patronised in the average Highland parish. Few *Gaelic* books of any kind are read. Not only is the number of Gaelic books available small, but there are many Gaelic-*speaking* persons quite unable to *read* Gaelic. This latter fact accounts for the lingering custom of "reading the line" in psalm-singing where Gaelic is preached. This reference to psalm-singing reminds us that among a large proportion of Highlanders there is a strange prejudice against anything else than *psalms* being sung in church. They virtually discard paraphrases; and as for *hymns*, they would shudder at the thought of singing them. Some years ago a minister in a Highland parish "gave out" a paraphrase in church, and had scarcely done so when an old elder of the congregation, greatly moved by the dreadful innovation, said, loud enough to be heard by all in church, "I wonder is the *psalms* o' Dauvid all done?"!

Few Gaelic books are read, we said. Those that are read, as a rule, are the works of Bunyan, Baxter, and Boston, comprising the well-known 'Pilgrim's Progress,' Baxter's 'Saints' Rest,' and Boston's 'Fourfold State,' all these translations having long enjoyed considerable popularity in the Highlands. Of works originally composed in Gaelic, the Hymns of Dugald Buchanan and Peter Grant in the golden age of Gaelic-speaking were very popular with many; but, as is true of all other Gaelic books, those that to-day read them are few compared with twenty years ago. 'Ossian,' of course, holds an honoured, a revered place in every Highland home where there is the least effort after a library; but 'Ossian,' even, is to-day rarely read in Gaelic. 'Caraid Nan Gaidheal' ('The Highlander's Friend'), a Gaelic work by the Rev. Dr Macleod, an eloquent Gaelic scholar and genuine Highlander, father of the late deeply lamented excellent man and eloquent preacher, Norman Macleod of Glasgow, has long been popular in various districts of the Highlands. It includes dialogues, many of them very clever and highly amusing, short essays of an instructive kind, and sermons betokening a clear head and large heart.

Gaelic song-books are not in large demand, and it is a pretty significant fact that there are many Highland parishes where a Gaelic song is to-day rarely heard. Here, again, the railway, the newspaper, and the spread of schools are telling powerfully. Although the poetry of an *ideal* Highland parish would not be reckoned anything like complete without Gaelic songs, sung at even by the milkmaid, and in the family circle in the long winter evenings, Gaelic songs are yielding to the general change. The love-songs, the martial airs, and the laments that, in days of yore, spoke to Highland hearts in the familiar accents of the Gaelic tongue, though their sentiment will long endure, must tend towards having an existence only in the fond recollection of those that have once heard them.

Besides those enumerated, there are other Gaelic publications known in the Highlands, some original, but most of them translations; but in respect of the limited and still diminishing reading of Gaelic, these latter publications need not be spoken of at any length. Some of them are religious songs, many of them are of the so-called sentimental order, while a few are of the martial kind, and others are laments. Various of these are well composed, by genuine Celts, good men and true; but even the best of such works are being read by a diminishing number,—a fact caused by a tide, the advance of which it were vain to try to check. So much for Gaelic books and Gaelic reading. Now for the English element in the literature in ordinary use in the average Highland parish of to-day.

A remarkable change of recent years is the now large and growing use of the newspaper. Some thirty years ago, though the population was then as large as now, not more than half-a-dozen newspapers came to Stratheden. To-day nearly thirty times that number come weekly to the parish, all eagerly waited for. No doubt the half-dozen of other days did duty for many readers, as those that got them, ordinarily the parsons, the "big fairmers," and the schoolmaster, gave a reading of the paper to one or more neighbours. At the same time, for every newspaper reader of thirty years ago in Stratheden, there are to-day at least fifteen readers.

The 'Inverness Courier,' lately grown into a tri-weekly from being a weekly paper, was then, as to-day, popular. Wisely moderate in its political attitude, and in every way respectably and judiciously conducted, the 'Courier' still holds its ground, and notwithstanding the growing circulation of daily papers in the Highlands, by means of which much of the news given in weekly, bi-weekly, or even tri-weekly papers is anticipated, in very many homes in Highland parishes the 'Courier' is to-day cordially welcomed. Another paper, the 'Northern Chronicle,' established apparently for the purpose of advocating moderate Conservative views, has recently appeared in Inverness. Its prudently mild tone and general "get up" promise well. The 'Weekly Scotsman' and 'People's Journal,' the latter also a weekly, are the papers having the largest circulation in Stratheden. Some six dozen of each arrive every Friday evening for regular subscribers. The former is very popular, on account of the great variety of its news, its well-arranged summaries, and its minute detailing of events of exciting interest. The 'People's Journal' is also popular in Stratheden, and that very much because of its stories or tales, of a kind leaning towards the sensational, but, generally speaking, with a healthy bettering tendency. Ploughmen and farm-servants generally read the 'People's Journal.' It gives considerable space to subjects affecting their interests, and its appreciation of the general circumstances of this class seems intelligent and reasonable. The 'Northern Ensign,' a weekly paper, published in Wick, is also read in Stratheden. It is smartly conducted, showing great variety, but devoting special attention to matters affecting the agricultural and fishing populations. Then there is 'The Highlander,' a paper started some dozen years ago in Inverness, with the special view of supporting the claims of the Gaelic language, and of awakening a practical interest in matters affecting Highland crofters. Though, however, its name and professed objects would lead to the belief that it meets with general acceptance in the Highlands, the circulation of 'The Highlander' is by no means large. The fact that, with one exception, the other papers referred to were established before 'The Highlander's' day began, will partly account for this; and the special attention given to the Gaelic language in 'The Highlander,' much though some may appreciate it, will not, we suspect, increase its circulation, for reasons we have already indicated when discussing the prospects of Gaelic as a spoken language. It may be added that, although the interests of the crofter receive special attention in 'The Highlander,' there are other papers circulated in the Highlands, papers of older standing than 'The Highlander,' that discuss this matter in its various aspects, generally in a calm and unprejudiced manner, so that the former cannot be said to have a monopoly of the subject.

Such are the newspapers ordinarily read in Stratheden. Their general circulation began with the extension of the railway to the parish some fifteen years ago. One or two of the shopkeepers receive parcels of the newspapers weekly, and for an hour or two after their arrival the shops are crowded with persons longing to get their paper. Some in the parish—the two parsons, the "big fairmers," and a few others—get a daily paper. There is no *Highland* "daily." Nor can this be felt to be a serious want. The Scotch dailies, such as the 'Scotsman,' 'Courant,' 'Review,' and 'Glasgow Herald,' may be had in the greater number of Highland parishes on the evening of the day of publication, and in some of them early in the afternoon. Of course there are many parishes in the West and North Highlands not yet thus favourably situated; but telegraphic communication is now becoming so general, that, in specially exciting times, there is a compensating element for the absence of an early arrival of the daily newspaper.

Speaking of newspapers, there are others than those mentioned that are circulated in certain districts of the Highlands—namely, two Aberdeen dailies, the 'Inverness Advertiser,' the 'John O'Groat Journal,' the 'Oban Times,' the 'Ross-shire Journal,' 'Perthshire Advertiser,' and the 'Invergordon Times;' but it is not necessary here to do more than allude to these.

It is a remarkable and melancholy fact that books, and indeed literature in almost every form, were virtually forbidden by some of the Highland clergy of about forty years ago, and an even later period. The reason for this is not clear, though there seems to be ground for the unpleasant suspicion that the clergy, finding the ignorance of the people enabled them to perpetuate their clerical sway and foster general intolerance, dreaded the revolution of enlightenment which reading habits might bring about. Strange to say, an occasional survival of the effects of this dark tyranny may even to-day be met with. There is a crofter in a Highland parish, not thirty miles from Stratheden, who is understood to doubt the propriety of perusing literature generally, and especially newspapers, on the plea that the latter are "awful worldly." The reader will not be surprised to hear, marvellous though the question is, that this crofter is said to have lately inquired of a neighbour whether the Pope belonged to the Free or the Established Church! It would be interesting to know what his Holiness of the Vatican would think of this Highland crofter's very limited acquaintance with ecclesiastical distinctions.

Newspapers constitute the chief reading of the great bulk of the people of Stratheden, and this is true of many Highland parishes. Libraries are rare, because reading habits, though decidedly growing, are not yet prevalent. Besides newspapers some read such books as 'The Pilgrim's Progress,' 'Tales of a Grandfather,' books of sacred and secular songs, 'The Celtic Magazine,' a very well conducted monthly published in Inverness; and the cheap literature, in the form of novels, biographies, and narratives of travel in foreign lands, is also, in the average Highland parish, beginning to be largely used. Of course in some Highland parishes—those having more or less important villages—there is a good library, and no small number of readers. With the extended educational machinery of to-day, and the additional enlightenment caused by travel, reading habits must grow; and though, as in other places, some in Highland parishes will have an appetite for literature not elevating or in any way healthy, the general result must be to promote liberal-mindedness and Christian charity,—qualities not hitherto so prominent in certain quarters of the Northern Highlands as the friends of true progress could have wished.

CHAPTER V.

MANSES AND MINISTERS IN A HIGHLAND PARISH OF TO-DAY.

THERE was a time, prior to the memorable Secession of '43, when the designation "manse" applied to one house only in a Highland parish. It is not so now, of course, there being to-day two houses that go by the name of manse—the homes of the pastors of the Established and Free Church congregations respectively.

We take the Established Church manse as the representative habitation, giving it, as is most due, the precedence belonging to age; and if we speak of the reverend occupant of the more venerable abode before making any observations regarding his reverence "over the way," this is because it might tend to confusion of ideas were the minister dissociated from his manse.

The parish manse of Stratheden is an ancient

enough fabric, and has a very *past* sort of look about it. It has seen all this century's changes, and stood the storms of twenty winters before the century began. The manse and church literally *stand high* in the parish, being set upon a hill; and we have heard the parish minister—who, by the way, has no Ritualistic leanings—say that a friend lately teased him upon his *high* Church surroundings.

The parish minister of Stratheden — the Rev. George Cameron—is a comparatively young man; and while a first look gives the impression that he is of a cheerful disposition—"too happy like for a munnistarr," as some of the older natives have been heard to say—a discerning unprejudiced look discovers a reasonable measure of professional gravity in his expression.

Mr Cameron leads an active life. Not that his pastoral duties can be called arduous; for, as is the case in many Highland parishes of to-day, the comparative smallness of the congregation precludes this supposition. An energetic earnest man, however, will always find plenty useful work to do. Mr Cameron, though not eager to take a prominent part in extra-professional work, is a member of the School Board and of the Parochial Board of the parish. In the latter he sits *ex officio ;* and in almost all Highland parishes—the rural ones especially, by pretty general consent—it is considered right that the "paercesh munnistarr" should be a member of the School Board, in the deliberations of which latter body Mr Cameron should be able to offer some specially useful suggestions. He has himself been a schoolmaster for a considerable time, and the benefit of his experience should be felt. It is worthy of notice that very many of the Highland clergy of both denominations have been school teachers before or during their university training for the ministry. In most instances "exchequer" requirements explain this fact; while in a few cases the desire to be employed induces the aspirant to the sacred office to take teaching in a school, or become tutor in a private family, during the vacation of the summer and autumn months. The Education Act of 1872 will go far to remove this long-prevalent feature in the history of the Highland clergy. It gives little or no countenance to the idea of a *substitute* teacher during *the* teacher's absence at the university; and thus, doubtless, the practice alluded to will soon cease to hold.

Regularity in pastoral visitation would appear to be highly prized by the average Highlander; for, whether or not there is a genuine wish to see "the munnistarr" at their homes, loud and sometimes bitter comments are made on those of the clergy that are thought to neglect the practice. The older people speak more strongly, and very probably with greater sincerity, on this matter. The two parsons of Stratheden seem to *visit* frequently. His reverence of the Auld Kirk has not so much to do in this way; and if his congregation had strong faith in the virtue of frequent visiting, it would be easy enough for him to meet their views in this respect: not that his congregation is very small, though we have heard him say he could wish it larger. Many of the Established Church congregations in the Highlands are small; but in several cases there has been an increase within recent years.

Useful as the two pastors of a Highland parish of to-day may be in their day and generation, time was when, in a more especial manner than now, the minister was "guide, philosopher, and friend" to his flock. As a rule, "a man he was to all the country dear:" and if the stipend was not at quite so slender a figure as "forty pounds a-year," the frequent calls on the minister's purse, and the generous giving practised by many, left often enough but a very attenuated balance on the right side at the year's end. Some forty years ago the minister often gave *legal* advice, not seldom *medical* prescriptions, to his people, and thus lightened the sheriff's duties and curtailed the doctor's bills. No doubt, even to-day, instances of this extra-professional work may be met with, especially in the matter of medical prescriptions. But doctors are becoming more numerous in the Highlands; and as for the legal advice, the people seem fonder of going to "see the Shurra aboot it," and this latter dignitary now hears not a few of a certain kind of causes in which, in other days, the minister attempted, and often with success, to act the part of peacemaker. In short, the relation between the minister and people in a Highland parish of to-day is neither so close nor so firm as it was some forty or fifty years ago, and especially before the Secession of '43. Reasons for the change will probably occur to the reader.

As a rule, the staff of domestics in the parish manse of to-day is not quite so large as was the case some fifty or even twenty years ago. In those days the manse kitchen was a largely peopled place. In addition to the ordinary servants there was the old woman who presided at the spinning-wheel,—a very important personage in the days when woollen manufactories were unknown in the Highlands. She was a great favourite with the young people of the manse, by whom she was in some cases familiarly called "Granny Spinning." She could spin more than one kind of *yarn*, and had many stories the little ones liked to hear. She often combined the management of the poultry with spinning, and was indeed willing to make herself generally useful. There is now no room for this follower of other days. Her chief occupation is gone: homespun fabrics are daily becoming more unfashionable. Woollen manufactories are being established in Highland parishes—there is one in Stratheden—and Granny Spinning's winter work can now be overtaken at the mills in a few hours. Hence this retainer of a Highland manse will soon be known to history alone.

There is another retainer of other days now comparatively unknown. We refer to those half-witted, harmless persons taken into manses from charitable motives, and who were ordinarily employed in herding cattle, running messages, and helping generally about the manse or glebe. It would seem—to the regret of many kind-hearted ones by no means foes of progress—as if most of these persons nowadays found their way to poorhouses and other parochial institutions as people needing supervision.

"The minister's man," of course, still endures.

He is a permanent institution, and a person of very considerable self-importance. The parson, generally speaking, is not particularly strong in the knowledge of farming; and when this is the case, where there is a suitable *man*, the glebe management is intrusted to the latter, the sense of responsibility thus imparted giving an air of self-importance to the *man's* general bearing. Then he is, as a rule, the kirk officer, which likewise helps to make him a person of consideration. The Stratheden parish minister's man is somewhat of a character. James Morison—this is the man's name—is a little man with an air not little. He seems fond of hearing himself talk; but as he is fond of working,—James is a very diligent workman, often first done with spring and harvest work in the parish,—his propensity for talking is overlooked by those most interested. James is kirk officer in the parish church, and discharges his duties with commendable precision. From certain observations we have heard, it appears that some of his Sunday duties entail a considerable facial strain on James. The normal aspect of his physiognomy is not one suggestive of gravity, or one that speaks of placidity; but it is well known that James on the Sunday, while acting beadle, and especially while gathering " the collection " with the ladle, looks a very model of calm gravity and official propriety.

There is another of the manse staff that deserves a passing notice—Thomas Macleod, a party of some thirty years of age, and somewhat of an original character. When quite a boy he came to the manse in the capacity of herd, and was subsequently promoted to the post of general farm-servant. Being "a quate lad," and a faithful servant, Thomas, in respect of his originality, has been much "made of," a consequence of which is that a certain familiarity in addressing superiors falls to be enumerated among his peculiarities. Referring at family worship one evening not many weeks ago to the pool of Siloam, his reverence was somewhat amused, if not startled, by hearing Thomas abruptly volunteer the observation, "There's a well like that in oor place,"—the reference being to a well in Thomas's native parish supposed to possess miraculous powers of healing.

Thomas is one of the now rapidly diminishing number that are more at home in Gaelic than in English, notwithstanding that he affects a preference for the latter. An instance of this preference for English-speaking, and, at the same time, of his wish to be thought clever,—Thomas, like many others, is very vain in this respect,—is worth repeating. We had the facts from the parish minister of Stratheden. The minister and a brother clergyman were one day not long ago driving from the manse to the railway station. Thomas accompanied them in the capacity of driver. Mr Cameron, finding the train would very soon be due at Stratheden, by way of a hint to Thomas as to the driving rate desirable, remarked, "I hope we have time enough." Thomas, who, it seems, thought the reverend gentlemen might have left the manse a little sooner, gravely replied, "Indeed am no sure aboot it. 'Time wull no wait for tide nor for no man'!" Both parsons were nigh convulsed with laughter at poor Thomas's rendering of the well-known proverb; but it may be the latter interpreted the laughter as a compliment to his cleverness and *correct* quotation.

The Reverend Norman Nicolson, Free Church Minister of Stratheden, like his brother of the Auld Kirk, is a comparatively young man. Otherwise, so far as appearance goes, they seem unlike each other. The Free Kirk parson, to look at him, seems sombre, gloomy even, while his reverence of the Established Church would appear to be cast in a livelier, happier mould. We have heard, however, some that know Mr Nicolson say that at home he is not particularly, if at all, sombre,—that *there* he seems cheerful; and we ourselves—it is our privilege to number the reverend gentleman among our acquaintance—have more than once seen that he can enjoy a joke, and even tell what some of his people would call a *worldly* story. The austere look that at times seems to grow on Mr Nicolson's countenance is not, however, unfavourable to his popularity with a certain section of his people. In referring to the facial contrast the two parsons present, one of the older natives, an adherent of the Free Church, commenting on some jocular remark the "Moaderat munnistarr" made to a neighbour he met on the road lately, said, "Och, munnistarrs shouldna be making people laugh; it's no for laughing they're int. Look at the soalam face Messtur Neeculsan hess; try wull *he* be laughing." The older native residents reckon a cheerful face as incompatible with clerical sanctity, and who knows but Mr Nicolson and some others are aware of this—who knows, indeed, but the fact has some sort of influence upon them in the matter of the regulating of their *facial* aspect?

The Rev. Norman Nicolson is believed by many to be what is called a diligent pastor, visiting his flock regularly, and endeavouring to provide what he considers suitable pabulum for Sunday instruction. His brother of the Established Church is likewise, to all appearance, entitled to be called a diligent pastor, though, so far as diligence in pulpit preparation is concerned, it is not so easy to compare the two parsons. Assuming that both are endowed with even an ordinary amount of brain-power, the Sunday duties cannot necessitate any considerable effort. For merely learned discourses, or for sermons demanding sustained thoughtful attention, the average resident is not greedy. In fact, among the older natives generally, anything savouring of research or independent thinking would not be appreciated. The sort of criticism, indeed, one hears now and then made on preaching and preachers is slightly peculiar. If the preacher think it necessary for clearness to make a few historical allusions to persons and places, many will say, "There was too much *husstary* there the day." Length and loudness seem to have a charm for not a few; and by a certain section of the Free Church community a hit at the "Moaderats" is reckoned admirable spicing in a sermon. A few years ago we attended the services in a certain Free Church, and the preacher discoursed in Gaelic for *two* hours, the Gaelic service alone—there was more to follow in English—occupying three and a half hours! To this day we feel inclined to yawn at even the recollection of the weariness of these long and long-remembered three and a half hours. Not so, however, with many that were there. As the audience dispersed, we overheard several speaking admiringly of the "grawnd *long* sairman we got the day. Some munnistarrs is too short wi' their sairmans in the day that's int." "Ah, he's a splendid preacher yon!" is another frequent comment; "you could hear him *fearful far away!*"

The intoned or "sing-song" style of preaching, practised chiefly by the older ministers of the Free Church, is popular with many, and we have heard some Free Church clergymen do it in a way rather pleasing to the ear. There was a sonorous, and soporific element in it which tended to place the hearer beyond the reach of the feeble and vague utterances often thus conveyed.

As to the matter of some of the discourses thus delivered, it is unnecessary to say much. Very often they are beyond the reach of ordinary criticism. An incident lately came under our notice, which may indicate the quality of the discourses of at least one disciple of the sing-song school,—one of the very few the Established Church can boast of. The Communion was being observed in a Highland parish, and a clergyman from a neighbouring parish, a person strong in the gift of *intonation*, was officiating. Another minister from a distance was present, and this latter, being unavoidably detained, did not arrive at the church until the preacher had proceeded some length with his discourse. Naturally desirous to know the text, he indicated his wish to the pastor of the church—a shrewd, clever man, not of the sing-song order—who was sitting beside him. The latter simply handed the stranger a Bible, at the same time whispering, "Open *anywhere!* it's all the same!" Many impartial observers are of this reverend gentleman's opinion, that discourses thus delivered are remarkable chiefly for the *extent* of ground they go over.

Mr Nicolson, the Free Church minister of Stratheden, is known more as a lengthy preacher than as one given to loudness or intonation, though by no means despising the two latter qualifications. Although, however, some of the younger Free Church clergymen think it right to imitate the style of certain Highland divines of other days, many of whom are celebrated among impartial people for the length, loudness, and narrowness of their preaching, a healthier sentiment is beginning to make its presence felt in a growing "sweet reasonableness."

The Rev. Norman Nicolson, it is said, speaks occasionally against the "Moaderats" in the course of his ordinary pulpit ministrations. It pleases some people, the older ones especially, and that in itself is a very important matter. This practice was much in vogue at, and long after, the Secession of '43, but, while always a foolish practice, must to most people sound terribly out of date at this time of day. Such weak displays are happily much rarer now than thirty, or even fifteen, years ago, but they must become rarer still as enlightenment spreads. Pulpit attacks of this sort may be convenient when the preacher has nothing else to say, and the orthodox *time* has not been made up, and they may be resorted to in the effort to satisfy a certain local estimate of Christian charity; but, fortunately, forces are marching along that must tend to sweep away the silly, if not cowardly, practice. All Highland Free Church clergymen, happily, are not alike in this respect. Some of them — earnest, thoughtful men, who have breathed a healthier, brighter, religious atmosphere, and who undoubtedly practise a manlier, more useful preaching—are sorry enough for the feeble and vulgar intolerance of certain of their brethren.

The Free Church minister of Stratheden is a member of the Parochial and School Boards; and representing, as the Free Church does, so large a proportion of the people, it is proper that its ministers should have a voice in such business. The Established Church clergy in most Highland parishes are also members of these Boards; and though ordinarily the latter minister to a minority of the ratepayers, not a few of these ratepayers are sensible enough to look at the Auld Kirk parson's qualifications for office apart altogether from the *ecclesiastical* question, within which limits people of greater pretensions to culture and wisdom unfortunately too often refuse to confine themselves. We are glad to understand that the Rev. George Cameron, parish minister, and the Rev. Norman Nicolson, Free Church minister of Stratheden, get along with a pleasing measure of harmony at the meetings of these Boards. It is said that some little sectarian displays do occur, and we have also heard it stated who, as a rule, the aggressor is; but, as it is just possible this latter allegation may come from a prejudiced source, we do not lay too much stress upon it. When the qualifications of candidates for a vacant school in the parish are being considered, we have heard people who ought to know say that the clerical School Board members manifest a readiness to be influenced by sectarian considerations, and this gives rise to a little *feeling*. But of the clergy even, people should not expect too much.

We referred to the comparative harmony apparently subsisting between the two parsons of Stratheden. It is strange, sad indeed, that such a fact should require to be specially noted. But so it is. In too many Highland parishes these *brethren* do *not* dwell in unity, though preaching brotherly love and kindness. We know of a parish not fifty miles from Stratheden where the Free Church minister will not *speak* to his "brother" of the Established Church— will not even return the compliment of the common courtesy of bowing, with which the Auld Kirk parson salutes his brother of the Free Church. No one seems to know the reason. The Free Kirk parson is said by many to be a *good* man, and the "Moaderat munnistarr" in question is also believed, by Free Church people, as well as by members of his own congregation, to be a very estimable character. Why will the Free Church parson not speak, not even bow, to his brother? Some say it is envy,—something regarding the "steepand," as the people call it, and the "*poseeshan* (position) o' the Moaderat munnistarr;" but surely there must be more than that in it. One day last autumn, these two clergymen, going in opposite directions, happened to be crossing a bridge. They *must* meet. Here was a terrible dilemma for his reverence of the Free Church. Fortunately, as the latter no doubt believed, a means of *escape* appeared. A ship lay fastened to a pier close to the bridge,—had lain there indeed for many weeks previously. The Free Church clergyman knew the name of that ship very well, but to let his fellow Christian of the other denomination pass, he turned his back to the latter and bent down as if eager to know the name of the ship! and thus the *terror* passed. A member of the Free Church in the district witnessed the scene, and *understood* it. Meeting the Established Church minister a few minutes after the Free Church minister's devout bend, the witness referred to said, "Oh, dear me! yon work was awful!"

Many instances of this contemptible sort of feeling might be given, but it is not a pleasant theme, and we pass from it in the hope and belief that such weak and cowardly displays will, not long hence, be swamped in the grand results of time. The younger clergy of the Free Church are not so prone to such displays of feeling, although, for fear of offending certain of the older and more bigoted ones among their people, they cannot well afford, as some of themselves say, to fraternise much with their brethren "over the way."

We referred to the commendable regularity with which the Free Church minister of Stratheden visits his flock. Certain persons, adherents of the other denomination very probably, allege that the frequency and regularity of Free Kirk pastoral visits are greatly prompted by the hope that the visit may result in increased contributions to the Sustentation Fund. Without inquiring as to how much, if any, uncharitableness there is in the insinuation, it should be noted that the efforts and success of the Free Church, in this matter of the Sustentation Fund, deserve all praise; and many persons are of opinion that not a few Established Church people might well imitate the habit of *giving* it has called forth. We suspect, however, the *cheerful* giving to the said fund, so far at least as Highland parishes are concerned, is not so prevalent as some would wish it to be believed.

It would further appear there is no authoritative law against receiving a contribution to this fund from others than Free Church people. If there be, we know of a case where it was disregarded in a sheepish sort of way. A farmer, an adherent of the Established Church, was buying sheep some three or four years ago from another farmer, who belonged to the Free Church, in the same parish. The seller demanded sixpence a-head more than the purchaser would give, and they could not, or would not, strike a bargain. Ultimately a happy thought seized the Free Church party—the seller—and he said to the purchaser, "Well, well, will you do this? if you'll not give me that sixpence"—meaning sixpence a-head, which would come to about thirty shillings—"give me a pound-note for the Sustentation Fund, and the sheep are yours!" The Established Church dealer consented. He wanted the sheep, and it was so far a gain—about ten shillings—assuming the seller would hold out, and he gave the pound-note—to the Sustentation Fund! The collector for the district annually thereafter called at the house of the Established Church party for his contribution to the fund, and never, we understand, went in vain.

We hinted that the manse is not to-day so great a centre of influence as of yore. This change, so far, was inevitable, seeing the Secession of '43 divided the people. There are cases, of course, where both manses in a Highland parish of to-day exercise a very considerable influence for good. There are not a few Highland manses in which intellect and art are well represented; and we know of some manses, of both denominations, where "the feast of reason and the flow of soul" make their brightening, bettering influences felt. The success of many "sons of the manse" of a Highland parish in one or other of the learned professions, as well as in other departments of life, is a tribute to the excellence of the atmosphere breathed in early days; and in many Highland parishes of to-day, the daughters of the manse will be found equal at least in the usual accomplishments to some that make greater pretensions, and superior to many that have had greater advantages of a financial kind.

Sometimes, however, it will happen that the wife of the manse, or even the daughter, and where neither wife nor daughter is, the sister of the minister, may be of a disposition not calculated to strengthen the kindly feeling that should exist between pastor and people. She may be, and now and then is, a gossip, and this tends to bring about certain unpleasantnesses. Such a one soon gathers local news of various kinds, at times neither edifying nor even reliable. She makes the acquaintance of certain of her own sex, who frequent the manse with *stories*. The minister cannot help hearing some of these. He may even wish to hear them. Nay, he may be sanctioning, if not enjoining, this method of hearing the local news, and he may even make certain rumours thus circulated the subject of comment on the Sunday,—a result not always favourable to the growth of pure and undefiled religion in his congregation.

We are glad, however, to think such cases do not form the rule, though undoubtedly they exist. In certain high places connected with one of the two denominations ordinarily represented in a Highland parish of to-day, there was, not long ago, a melancholy complaint uttered as to the qualifications of certain aspirants to the office of the holy ministry in the denomination in question. The complaint was followed by the expression of the hope that representatives of a *better* class would become more numerous. It should, of course, be no disparagement to a man that he is of poor parentage and limited means; and, indeed, many a humble cottage has contributed to the Church, and other professions, men that would be an honour to any home. At the same time, while gossips and busybodies are found among every class, it cannot be doubted that in proportion as the supply of clergymen is more drawn from among the liberally-brought-up class, the entanglements and unpleasantness occasioned by taking gossip to the manse will become less frequent.

There was a time when the average native resident was afraid to "say anything aboot the munnistarr." It was not considered "canny," the parson being believed to be either beyond criticism, or one whom it was best to let alone. This superstitious belief is dying out. To-day no one in the parish is more freely commented on than the minister, every one seeming to have a right to say what he should be and do, and even say. His preaching, his outgoings and incomings generally, his style and manner of dress even, are subjected to pretty free, and sometimes unkind, if not unjust, criticism.

And yet to this day there linger traces of the undiscerning reverence of other days. Whatever weakness of temper or other uninviting peculiarity the minister may display, by some it is readily condoned with the observation, "Och, but he's a good quate man, and a very good man for all that!" A crofter's daughter in Stratheden, a sensible-looking young woman, rather amused us one day last winter by relating an incident illustrative of the sort of reverence alluded to. She was working with some others in the harvest-field on a certain day, and Angus M'Intosh, a lay preacher, and considered a *good* man, happened to be passing. Angus was prepared to address people on religious subjects on all occasions, and sometimes did so, it is said, unseasonably. On the occasion specified he expressed a wish to address these harvest workers, of which our informant was one. In the course of his address rain began to fall, and fell heavily; but this apparently sensible and intelligent young woman, in all seriousness, told us that, while the audience were nearly drenched with rain, not a drop fell on the lecturer's uncovered and equally unsheltered head! and she gravely added, " Indeed, it's likely the Lord put the rain past *him!*" While we cannot help, to some extent, appreciating the capacity for reverence this sort of feeling indicates, it cannot be supposed unpromising to find that such faith in the *privileges* of even " good" men is now exceeding rare. In the average Highland parish of to-day, the bulk of the people of both denominations, in consequence of the progress of general enlightenment, are more inclined for, and capable of, reasonable and independent criticism of men and opinions. While we are glad to believe that the feeling of reverence for what is sacred will continue to find as congenial a soil in Highland parishes as anywhere else, no wise friend of the Highland people will regret that such unthinking reverence as is illustrated by the incident just related, is being rapidly relegated to the region of exploded fancies.

CHAPTER VI.

HEATHFIELD HOUSE AND THE PEOPLE'S FRIEND.

HEATHFIELD is picturesquely situated among the majestic hills of Blackburn, in an upland district of Stratheden, and all around there reigns the calm repose of a grand solitude. The present tenant of Heathfield House and farm is the Honourable Arthur M'Alpine, heir of a noble Scottish house memorably and brilliantly associated with not a few of the more famous events of British history. Though seemingly a somewhat romantic choice, Arthur at a very early age adopted the profession of a farmer, and right well does he know his profession and attend to its requirements. It would not, perhaps, be difficult, among the nobility and various others of the wealthier classes of the country, to find some parents and friends who would rejoice—and with good cause—if some of the sons of the home would, like Arthur M'Alpine, turn their attention to useful work, such as farming, and thus not only learn the dignity of labour, but fall into the way of cultivating a healthful physical and moral life. Be this as it may, Arthur M'Alpine is a farmer from choice — very early choice, too, as has been said; and he himself likes to tell how some of his relatives teasingly call him the *Gentle* Shepherd,—sheep-farming being the department to which he specially devotes his attention.

Arthur loves work for its own sake, and his life is one of constant useful activity. He is too genuine, too sensible, to be ashamed to do any work that may turn up in the usual requirements of his profession; and though he works with his shepherds, they never forget his position—nor does he himself. They invariably, as do all others that know him, accord him that respect which they feel to be due to him for his noble qualities of head and heart, as well as for his rank. He, though, as is right, knowing his position, and the respect due thereto, is happily no empty boaster of nobility, and looks on his fellow-creatures as brother men having their feelings and their rights.

Though enthusiastic in his devotion to his calling

—carefully directing its minutest details, and lending a helping hand in the carrying out of the manual portion of the work—Arthur finds time for taking a share in the direction of parochial affairs generally. At first, when he came to reside in Stratheden, some six or seven years ago, he seemed disinclined to take any part in matters outside his farm. This, however, was not owing to any dislike to giving time and counsel in such matters — for indeed it seems to be his very nature to be doing good—but to a modest shrinking from putting himself forward, as if he merely wished to make himself officious. As chairman of the School Board, his shrewd practical way of looking at matters is of great value; and his excellent business habits and large-hearted intelligent interest in the best welfare of the community, justly entitle him to the high opinion entertained of him as a leader in matters affecting the management and prosperity of the parish.

The style of Arthur's immediate surroundings at Heathfield House is in keeping with the man. No vain display is visible—no feeble strivings after mere costly grandeur for its own sake. Everything in furniture and other household belongings is plain, yet elegant and rich. Usefulness and reasonable comfort have evidently been the objects aimed at in the general get-up of Arthur M'Alpine's home. Prominent among the wall decorations at Heathfield House are relics of Arthur's travels in foreign lands. He has travelled more than most men of his age— Arthur is not yet thirty—and his foreign reminiscences are often intensely interesting.

To spend an evening with Arthur M'Alpine in his sanctum at Heathfield House is a veritable treat. His smoking-room, in which we have been privileged to spend many a happy hour, is a cosy cabin, and the mere look of it readily makes one feel at home—more especially after a look at mine host's kindly face. Though much alone at home, his busy life affording but spare leisure for company, M'Alpine always entertains, and certainly seems entertained by, a large company of—ye haters of the feline tribe shudder not!—*cats* of various sizes, ages, and colours. Whether it is, as a clerical friend, with a deplorable weakness for punning, puts it, that Arthur M'Alpine entertains so many cats because he is fond of *mews*-ic; or whether it is that, like all of us, he has his peculiar fancy, which takes this shape,—it is not necessary to inquire; certain it is the cats are there. Happening to be at Heathfield one evening lately, we observed three of these *mews*-ical quadrupeds—as the parson referred to would say—in the smoking-room: one, a big, fat, and at-home-looking animal, purring contentedly on the floor; while the other two were indulging in a wrestling exercise, indicative of possibilities, if not probabilities, of positive warfare. Taking occasion to remark that he was well provided with cats, Arthur replied with a smile that these were only a *few* of them; and shortly afterwards—lo and behold!—cat after cat came gradually dropping in through an opening in one of the windows,—an arrangement specially designed by Arthur,—until, wonderful to relate, no fewer than *thirteen* cats occupied the floor! Some were purring in a reclining posture, some wrestling, some administering—old to young, or big to little—something of the nature of a castigation for some supposed or actual error, and one here and there indulged in an exercise of playfulness on its own account. The reason for this rather unusually large collection of cats seems to be that their play, with its manifold manœuvrings, its sly glances, its sudden pouncings, and its amusing collapses and disappointments, affords positive amusement and delight to mine host of Heathfield House.

Notwithstanding this fondness for *large gather-*

ings, Arthur is not particularly fond of company. No one, however, likes better to meet a few select friends occasionally, and in such a situation Arthur M'Alpine undoubtedly shines. His one great aim, evidently, is to make his visitors happy—to make them feel at home. Though by profession a farmer, he is quite up in other subjects; and, with great tact and good sense, he directs the conversation by turns into such channels as will suit the profession, or elicit the opinions, of the several individuals of the company.

Arthur is quite a master in the art of *teasing.* He is so pointed with it, and yet so generous, so gentlemanly, in short, that even those against whom his banter may be directed cannot but enjoy it. A few weeks ago we happened to be one of a few spending an evening at Arthur's hospitable home. Mr George Maxwell Hay, a young gentleman from the south of Scotland—a representative of a good old Scottish family, and a friend of Arthur's — was one of the company. He was staying at Heathfield, having come there for the purpose of getting some insight into sheep-farming,—and certainly in no better hands could he have been placed than in those of Arthur. The Rev. Mr Cameron, parish minister of Stratheden, was also one of the party. Somehow the parson and Hay got into a conversation about the now pretty venerable question of "the antiquity of the Gaelic language." The conversation was gradually assuming something of an argumentative turn, and M‘Alpine by this time was anxious to learn what it was all about,—not but that the reverend gentleman and young Hay were conducting the conversation in a perfectly friendly and agreeable manner. The parson, indeed, is not understood to be a contentious man, though, like most of us, he has considerable faith in his own opinions. Nor is Hay, to all appearance, an irritable or opinionative young man: on the contrary, he seems a most amiable, good-tempered youth. But Arthur M‘Alpine, being in *teasing* mood, thought here was a grand opportunity; and addressing Hay, he remarked: "Well, young man, are you really trying to enlighten Mr Cameron with some of your *mature* opinions? May I ask what the subject of conversation is?" "Oh yes," Hay readily replied; "it's about the Gaelic language,—about how old it is, and matters of that sort,—only we were not disputing. All that's in it is, that I don't quite feel sure if the language is so very old as some people imagine!" Arthur quite understood that Mr

Cameron was somewhat at home on this subject; and he knew, besides, that Hay did not pretend to have made the question a subject of anything like special study, so that mine host was intensely amused at the somewhat incongruous aspect of the supposed debate. "Oh, well, Hay," Arthur replied—the irony causing much laughter, in which Hay good-naturedly joined—"you know Mr Cameron cannot be supposed to know much about the matter; and as for your own attainments in that direction, why, you are of course quite learned in the question, and therefore it is pretty evident who must yield." The Rev. Mr 'Cameron, greatly enjoying Arthur's banter, and admiring Hay's apparently imperturbable good-nature, wound up the "debate" by remarking, that very probably on questions more practically useful than that of the antiquity of the Gaelic language, however philologically interesting, Mr Hay would yet be able, by a careful use of his talents, to pronounce a mature and sound opinion.

It is not alone to select friends that Arthur is kind: hospitality ever reigns at Heathfield House. The wandering wayfarer on begging bent never calls at Heathfield in vain. Arthur, beyond a doubt, has the blessings of the poor, and his name is a household word in the cottages of the crofters of Stratheden. The reader will soon see there is good cause why it should be so.

In common with other parts of Scotland, Stratheden felt the depressing sweep of the disastrous snowstorm of 1878-79. Large farmers and crofters alike suffered from the hardship and perplexity of the situation. The crofters' supplies of fodder were all but gone, before the storm—which lasted some twenty weeks—had half run its course. Provender in most cases was scarce, and so was money. Arthur M'Alpine was equal to the occasion. He was both able and willing to help, and, being a far-seeing young man, took time by the forelock. Soon after the snow showed signs of lingering, and when the local supplies of hay and straw were becoming alarmingly short, he, with his usual good sense, thought it might be better to provide for probabilities of the most bleak description. He arranged for bringing to Stratheden a supply of hay and corn sufficient to feed his flocks, even should the snowstorm last far into the spring; and at the same time leave a considerable margin of a surplus, wherewith — and Arthur's generous heart had this in view all along—to supply crofters and others with fodder for their cattle, and sheep, and horses.

The reader does not require to be told that Arthur was willing to help. He was eager, indeed, to be of use in the distressing anxiety of the hour, and gave decidedly practical and substantial evidence of this eagerness.

The Stratheden crofters well know that we are not exaggerating Arthur's praises. Were we to submit our observations to them, we feel sure they would say, "Oh, that's no near praise enough at all: put a lot more of praise in it." But, since we have not seen cause to ask them what to say, the reader must rest content with our unassisted estimate of Arthur's good qualities,—not an estimate, be it noted, of unmeaning praise, but one that, if erring at all, does so on the side of being under rather than over the mark.

The crofters' provender was becoming alarmingly scanty soon after '79 came in. To add to the anxiety of the situation, money was scarce—somewhat scarcer than usual. In the case of the Stratheden crofters, as already indicated, the potato crop, generally speaking, is a source of considerable income,—as is indeed the case with the crofters of most Highland parishes of to-day,—many of these crofters being able, out of the proceeds of the sale of this commodity, to pay their rent and have a surplus besides. The potato crop in the harvest immediately preceding the memorable winter referred to, however, was not a profitable one, returns being small and prices low—fifty per cent, indeed, lower than for some time previous.

Arthur M'Alpine ordered word to be sent to the Stratheden crofters that he would supply them with hay and corn at a cheap rate—so cheap, indeed, that it signified a considerable personal outlay to himself—to be paid whenever they were able. In order to understand the full extent of the kindness thus shown, it is proper to mention that on a previous occasion, after an unusually poor harvest, the same generous friend supplied large quantities of hay and corn, in many instances virtually a gift.

It may be as well to observe that the Stratheden crofters were in no way in more trying circumstances than those of other parishes. In ordinary years their circumstances are certainly as comfortable as those of any crofters in Scotland. Their noble landlord takes a kind-hearted, thoughtful interest in their welfare, and offers them considerable encouragement towards the improvement of their holdings. But the winter of 1878-79, as already explained, was an exceptionally trying one.

Arthur's message of kindness gladdened many a heart and home in Stratheden. From far and near—from the far-off heights of the parish, and from the most distant corners of the straths and glens—the crofters came to the Stratheden railway station, where Arthur's bounteous liberality was being given out,—one getting a bag of oats, another some hay, some both hay and oats; and none really needing help was sent empty away. "Be am beannachd dha'n sgire e!" (What a blessing he is to the parish!) we have heard more than one of the Stratheden crofters say of Arthur; and well might they say it.

When the strain of the anxiety of the season was beginning to give way, and when people, as it were, got time to think of all that took place, it occurred to many, as a very proper and desirable thing, that there should be some public recognition of Arthur's generosity. The matter merely required to be mentioned to be at once universally and enthusiastically taken up. Not a few, however, dreaded that the idea of any public display of such a kind would be distasteful to Arthur. It was well known he did good at the prompting of a generous heart, and not from the weak vain love of being spoken of. This was a preliminary difficulty. But the people were in earnest, and they would risk the difficulty. They concluded that he would not disappoint, not to say vex, them, and that, for once at least, he would overcome his dislike to such a public display, and yield to the hearty unanimous wishes of the people. Arthur did consent, simply because he knew the people were in earnest, and because he did not like to disappoint them. The acknowledgment of Arthur's kindness took the shape of a very handsome piece of silver plate—a salver with suitable inscriptions in Gaelic and English—a gold locket, and an address. The day of presentation came, and certainly no more memorable day stands in the annals of the parish. The place of meeting, capable of holding several hundreds, was crowded, and the utmost enthusiasm prevailed. Old and young were there; and many came that rarely, if ever, countenance public gatherings. All were evidently bent on testifying their gratitude to the hero of the hour. Mr Malcolm Macgregor, the farmer at Burnside, was chairman, and he did his duty well, remarking how happy and proud he felt at being present at such an interesting gathering. The two parsons of the parish—the Rev. George Cameron, parish minister, and the Rev. Norman Nicolson, Free Church minister—were also there. They both, as was most meet, took a sort of lead in the matter; and while it is not our business to inquire what measure of regard the two reverend gentlemen cherish for each other, it was highly gratifying to see them co-operating in promoting a meeting got up to do honour to a genuine friend of the parish at large. Mr Nicolson read the address, the parish minister made the presentation, and both made suitable speeches.

The presentation having been made, Arthur M'Alpine rose to address the audience, and was, of course, most enthusiastically received. His speech was—like himself—sensible and genuine, and it was very pointedly expressed. He thanked the people of Stratheden for their handsome present, and modestly added, with reference to the occasion of the meeting, that he had only done his duty. After referring to the trying times they were passing through, and saying that people should help each other according to their ability, he expressed the hope and belief that better times would soon come. At the conclusion of his remarks a most enthusiastic and prolonged burst of applause made the place of meeting ring and ring again from floor to ceiling. So excited were the people with the enthusiasm of the occasion, that persons who, in ordinary circumstances, would shudder at the mere thought of being called on to make a speech, were actually impatient to hold forth, so as to add their testimony to the universal feeling of sincere gratitude to Arthur M'Alpine. William Sutherland, an old native resident—rarely, if ever, present at any public gathering except such as is of an ecclesiastical nature—was one of the audience, and there was no mistaking the fact that William wished to speak. In this there was something almost alarming to those who knew William and his usual ways. He is a shrewd enough old man, having a considerable endowment of pawky common-sense, but with some marked prejudices of a past age deeply rooted in him, such as a sort of, perhaps envious, dislike to fraternise with or countenance "big fairmers," and a doubt as to the propriety of any public gatherings of what William would call a worldly nature—that is, not specially religious. But on this occasion—and it is a pretty clear proof of how the universal heart of Stratheden was moved by Arthur's kindness—William overcame his prejudices, and was present. More than that, William wished to speak, and accordingly rose to address the audience. When William's voice was heard, great astonishment seized the greater number of those present, and some, especially of the younger people, as young people will do, giggled somewhat. The older natives, however, were proud of William, and admired his pluck. Some of the latter were heard to say, "Weel done, William Sutherland; surely them young men needna keep all the speakin' for themselves; and," added they, with a touch of local patriotism, "there are strenjars speaking here the day, and surely one o' oorselves micht speak for Stratheden as well as any strenjar." "Them munnistarrs," some of the less reverent were heard to say, "are kind o' like as if nobody could say a word at all but them. Some o' us canna preach a sermon, of coorse; but surely some o' us can speak for all that, whatever."

It was evident from the first that public speaking was not a matter with which William was familiar. He discarded the usual and ordinary preliminaries of addressing the chair, and respectfully announcing his presence to the audience. He may have intended to do what was right and proper, but very probably forgot it in the excitement of the rather novel situation in which he found himself. Indeed we have reason to believe the omission was unintentional—for the natives of Stratheden, like Highlanders generally, have a sort of instinctive politeness about them, instances of which the observer of their ways cannot fail to take notice of. William began by saying: "A'm no a speaker, and I canna speak, but a'm prood to be here, and a'm an ould man in the paereesh; and we should all thank the Giver of all good for giving to the paereesh such a freend as Maister M'Alpine. He's there himself, and a'll say this; a'm thinking the people o' Stratheden—and so they should—are thinking more of Maister M'Alpine than of any other body in the place; and," added William, giving a knowing glance towards the Rev. Mr Nicolson, his own minister, " a'm sure they are thinking more of Maister M'Alpine than they are of Maister Neeculsan here. It's a mercy Proavidence put in his heart the kindness that's in't, and that Maister M'Alpine, the noble young man, is making such a wise good use of his money." Great applause followed the close of William's remarks, and he himself looked as if he felt he had made a bold successful venture. There were other speeches: persons ordinarily not likely to dream of speechifying became eloquent under the inspiration of the universal enthusiasm, and they would have their say. All were grateful—genuinely so; all felt proud that the parish had such a friend, and that Stratheden could turn out such a large, respectable-looking gathering. And at the close of the proceedings a very decided mark of the popular enthusiasm was seen. As the crowd had been retiring, Arthur's carriage was coming towards the door, when, after the briefest deliberation, the horses were unyoked, and Arthur having taken his seat, off went the carriage at a splendid rate, drawn by a dozen or so of stalwart Stratheden Highlanders having willing hearts and strong arms, accompanied by a crowd, from which, at short intervals, a fresh contingent was supplied to drag the carriage along. They halted not until, over a steep and sometimes difficult road, five miles in length, they reached Heathfield House, the hospitable home of the Honourable Arthur M'Alpine, in the picturesque solitudes of Blackburn. Quite in keeping with the place and the hour, a Stratheden piper, playing appropriate airs, accompanied the procession all the way, and the proceedings ended with a hearty good Highland dance on the greensward in front of Heathfield House.

CHAPTER VII.

POPULAR ENTERTAINMENTS AND AMUSEMENTS IN A HIGHLAND PARISH OF TO-DAY.

ENTERTAINMENTS, beyond all dispute, are few and far between among us. In some few instances, such as in the central seaport of a fishing population, or other large village or small town, there may be musical, and other more or less intellectual, entertainments under the auspices of Young Men's Mutual Improvement Associations and similar societies; but in the general run of Highland parishes, the rural ones especially, there is a scantiness of popular means of amusement. For want of such, the younger members of the community often spend their evenings in shops and smithies, and the like, wasting precious hours, learning no useful accomplishment, but, on the contrary, in too many instances, acquiring decidedly unhopeful modes of speaking and thinking, and listening to local gossip, not seldom of a low and hurtful nature.

The reader will naturally ask if there is any reason why there should be such a dearth of the means of social improvement. In trying to answer this question, it must at once be admitted that those who might be expected to take a lead in providing such, have, in too many cases, prevented their existence—we mean the clergy, and other persons more or less ecclesiastical. Though the dawn of a better day is distinctly visible, it was too long the practice for the clergy to denounce, sweepingly and angrily, all sorts of entertainments or gatherings not exclusively for church purposes. They seemed to dread that the people should assemble themselves together anywhere than within the walls of a church—oblivious of the fact that if the providing of means of mental recreation and improvement were encouraged, there would be a clearer appreciation of such instruction as might happen to be supplied by the pulpit ministrations. Even to-day, if a concert is announced in a Highland parish, cases will be found where the clergy immediately thunder forth a wailing "encyclical" against the proposed profanity, and many angry words are uttered about "godless" amusements and the follies of the day; while any clergyman that openly countenances such gatherings is sure to be viewed with suspicion and displeasure by some of his flock. Not long ago there occurred in a Highland parish not very far from Stratheden a remarkable instance of the latter element of the peculiarity in question. In a small village in the parish referred to, some persons interested in the welfare of the district proposed to establish a coffee-room, with a view to which a concert was announced. Many of those coming in from the surrounding district to transact business in the village, when needing refreshment, must needs go to the only available place, the village inn; and, as some people in other than Highland parishes will do, certain of these would occasionally remain in the inn longer than was good for them. The promoters of the concert were anxious to remedy this state of matters, and hence the proposed establishment of a coffee-room. The proceedings at the concert began with the singing of the Hundredth Psalm, to the well-known tune of Old Hundred, which may be taken as evidence that no reckless, and still less profane, intentions actuated the promoters of the concert. Some secular songs of a popular kind, and incapable of offending the most fastidious, formed a part of the evening's programme. Among the audience there was the Free Church clergyman of the district—a fact which, while creditable to his good sense, marks him out as very different from the average northern Free Church parson. The concert was brought about for a most praiseworthy object, and surely those that are supposed to be set for doing good should countenance such efforts. But, reader, mark what follows! On the Sunday after the concert, lo and behold! some seats hitherto regularly occupied are seen to be vacant in the church where the pastor that was at the village concert is wont to preach. Some "weel-kent" faces are away, yea, even some long and solemn countenances long known as occupants of the upper seats in the local synagogue. Even among those in the said church on this particular day, here and there a face appears more sombre and elongated than was previously its wont, wearing an expression indicating doubtfulness as to the propriety, if not the safety, of sharing in the ministrations of the day. And why all this? wherefore these vacant seats and this doubting expression? It is because the clergyman in the pulpit is the same that countenanced the concert;—because, believing the coffee-room would help sobriety in the district, he was present at the concert got up to help in establishing it.

There is another species of entertainment that continues to call forth a severe rebuke from certain clerical monitors—to wit, balls, or what is understood to be dancing-parties ; an accompaniment of which, in addition to the music, is the effect of the liquor that possesses the almost marvellous power of cooling or warming as may be required.

A certain clerical gentleman, pastor of a Free Church congregation in a North-West Highland parish, not long ago allowed his zeal to outrun his discretion in rebuking the promoters of a ball. This pastor, seemingly alarmed for the safety of such of his flock as might think of going to the "awful gathering,"—or, as certain ill-natured ones of a different religious denomination insinuated, angry that the money spent on the ball was so much lost to the possible resources of the "collections" and Sustentation Fund,—made the ball the object of special and angry attack on the Sunday after he heard of it. The wails and denunciations of the enraged parson —though offensive to some of the younger and to the most of the intelligent portion of the congregation— greatly pleased the majority of the older people ; and old Duncan M'Gillivray, a member of the congregation, remarked, "Whatna grawnd sairman we got the day! The munnistarr give an awful blow to the pulpit; and them that's going to the ball got it the day." But poor Duncan was no dancer, nor had he an ear for music, and he liked the blow style of preaching. But the worst remains to be told. The pulpit warning, sad to say, moved not the hearts of the godless crew that promoted the ball, and the awful gathering took place.

On the evening of the ball, so much was the reverend gentleman's spirit troubled, that—horrible as well as wonderful to relate—he repaired to the ball-room; and there, *in propriâ personâ*, stood the parson, on that awful ball-room floor, it may well be believed, the observed of all observers. Some verily thought it was an apparition; and one or two persons, more given to levity than the others, wondered whether any wild intention of "tripping the light fantastic" had suddenly seized the reverend gentleman. But he himself soon set all surmising at rest by roaring at his loudest: "Stop this terrible work!" "Go out of this place, and shut the door of this awful place!" and kindred expressions. Melancholy to relate, the parson's roaring rebukes were unheeded. In reporting the ball to the newspapers read in the district, the local correspondent, with some sense of humour evidently, in giving some names after the usual " among those present we observed," mentioned the name of the Rev. Peter Mackay, the Free Church clergyman of the parish! It was, of course, too true. He could not deny he was at the ball. The angry parson now became afraid. What would his friends say? What would many that knew him think of him "among those present" at that godless amusement? It is gratifying, however, to be able to chronicle that the matter was satisfactorily settled —none that *knew* his reverence believing it was to sing or dance, or for any like profane purpose, he was among those present at the ball.

Another Free Church clergyman in a Highland parish—it is not very clear why the pastors of this particular denomination should specially shine in such capacities—placed himself, a very few years ago, in even a more ludicrous and alarming situation than did the Rev. Peter Mackay. We learned the circumstances from a member of his congregation, who heard the details from several persons who witnessed the scene. A marriage took place in the district, the officiating clergyman at which was the Rev. Neil Ferguson. In wedding festivities the bagpipes, as is yet generally the case, occupied a prominent place. It is important to note the presence of this musical instrument, because it "plays" an essential part in the story. The clergyman left after he had tied the nuptial knot; but happening, however, to meet the marriage-party at a later hour of the day, the piper playing an appropriate air, the Rev. Neil Ferguson, as if seized with temporary insanity, rushed up to the bagpipe-player—a young man of the district, and an adherent of the reverend gentleman's church—and violently wrenched the bagpipes from him, accompanying the act with angry mutterings about the godless music, and the foolish people, and like observations. Nor was this all. At the moment the pipes were forced out of the player's hands the bag was pretty considerably inflated, and as the parson held the pipes under his arm, the yet *unused* wind, in making its way out, made a sort of bagpipe-music, so that, beyond dispute, the parson was the bagpipe-*player* of the moment! There are, even at this moment, not a few of the clerical brethren of these angry parsons who have much the same narrow views anent rational amusements generally, but a growing public opinion is daily helping to render such scenes as those we have described less probable.

Stratheden shares in the too general scantiness of means of social and bettering entertainment. Nor is it easy to see why such is the case. Besides other persons that might reasonably be expected to help in providing something useful, there are two clergymen in the parish, and neither, so far as is known, in any remarkable way wanting in mental endowments and capabilities for general usefulness. In no Highland parish of to-day, it may be safely said, are the intellectual or other appliances so meagre but that, with some little energy and perseverance, such entertainments as penny readings, concerts, and popular lectures might be easily enough got up. These might also surely be so conducted as—instead of being institutions of which the clergy would be afraid—to be materially helpful towards promoting a healthy religious development among the community generally. The people *will* have excitement; and if, as unfortunately is the case the whole world over, some people in Highland parishes will go after excitement that is neither amusing nor healthy, those who assume the position of guardians of their morals should beware lest by a sour, unsympathetic denouncing of innocent rational entertainments and amusements, they may be virtually aiding in encouraging what they often have cause to deplore.

The places of public resort in Stratheden are not

numerous, and the most is made of such as do exist. For a long period, until within the past ten years, the habit of going to *ceilidh*—that is, visiting the neighbours' houses in the evenings—winter especially—for purposes of gossip, was largely patronised. Local events received the largest share of attention, but national questions were not altogether untouched; and some events, or *supposed* events, of the fable and ghost story order, were pretty largely laid under contribution. An intense craving for the surprising was very prevalent among the persons constituting this local parliament, and they who could satisfy this craving the best were the most popular frequenters of such gatherings. Personal observations, of course, of a kind uncomplimentary to some one or other in the neighbourhood, were often enough heard at the *ceilidh;* and sometimes the habit, unfortunately not peculiar to such meetings, of making free with the reputation of the absent, was more than sufficiently honoured. However, these gatherings had some harmlessly attractive features, and did good in a way. They kept the people from an idler and possibly worse way of spending their time; and before the state of matters to-day, when newspapers and books are so much more widely read, the *ceilidh* gathering in many instances was the means of circulating no small amount of useful intelligence. But the custom of *ceilidh* is rapidly disappearing, and the *ceilidh* meetings are to-day but thinly attended compared with even ten years ago. Railways and newspapers are tending to diminish the number at these gatherings, and not long hence, to all appearance, the *ceilidh* will cease to be known as a distinctive institution. The popular places of resort to-day are railway stations, blacksmiths', tailors', and shoemakers' shops, as also *the* shop by pre-eminence, or the general merchant's shop.

The first-named place—the railway station—seems a rather strange place to be regularly frequented except on business, and yet a considerable number of the young men and boys of Stratheden—as is the case in many other parishes—habitually frequent the railway station. One can easily understand how, at the time the train was a novelty, many old as well as young people would go to hear the snorting of the "each iarruinn" (iron horse), and see the huge load of waggons he dragged so rapidly in his train. But in Stratheden the charm of novelty has faded years ago, and still the people referred to, almost every evening, Sunday as well as week-days, from far and near, in all weathers, flock to the railway station. They all make a point, if possible, of being there at the arrival of the mail train from the south; and though few or none of them can have anything like an extensive correspondence, or any important or frequent business transactions, we have seen them pass towards the railway station shortly before train time running as if for dear life, afraid they would be too late. It is not easy to explain this phenomenon. It may be that the craving for excitement, incidental to the quiet monotony of the district, leads them to the railway station in the expectation of hearing something sensational among the latest intelligence; or it may be that some, even more curious, wish to see to whom a box or a parcel, or even a cask of sugar—and more especially, of something stronger—is addressed, such information being useful for purposes of gossip on some subsequent occasion. It is all very well to say that the station-master might prevent such gatherings. The Stratheden station-master is a highly efficient faithful official, and as capable at least as the average station-master of removing any annoyance that might exist; but the custom is deeply rooted, and it might not be judicious to deal summarily with it. The young people have few other places of public resort to go to; and though the gossip at these gatherings is not always elevating, it might seem hard, considering the fewness of places of amusement, to grudge the young men and boys this, as they must think, attractive entertainment.

The blacksmith's shop is a favourite resort, and many a remarkable conversation is heard in the "smithy"—many a strange sentiment is ventilated round the anvil. Angus Kennedy, the principal blacksmith in Stratheden,—to-day there are three in the parish, while twenty years ago there was but one,—is a man somewhat past middle life, with the brawny arm usually associated with the man of the anvil. He is altogether an intelligent person, and with that tendency to dictate and to be opinionative which the head of a place thus frequented is so apt to manifest. Many are they that visit, on business and without business, the smithy of Angus Kennedy. Crofters, grieves, and ploughmen generally, form of course the greater number. Not to speak of the attention paid to national affairs, no event of any consequence, or of no consequence, that takes place in or around Stratheden, fails to become a subject of comment among the frequenters of Angus Kennedy's "smithy." *Events* that never happened are occasionally discussed as well!—which latter, of course, is not peculiar to the blacksmith's or any other shop. "School boord and parochial boord maiters," as some of the assembled ones put it, are more or less exhaustively discussed; and the "school boord" elections of recent times created no small stir, the smithy parliaments taking special cognisance of the "maiter," and making somewhat remarkable comments both on the fitness of one or more of the "cawndidates" for membership in the "school boord," and on what the "boord," when elected, should do. "What the munnistarr said last Sawbath" is frequently very freely commented on; and special delight is felt in discussing some real or supposed *personal* admonitions or rebukes that may happen to be administered from one or both of the Stratheden pulpits.

Angus Kennedy, the smith, in virtue of his position as head of the house, is, of course, president of the anvil assembly; and, having seen a little of the world—Angus was in the south some years—greater deference is paid to his opinions, for the average native resident of a Highland parish looks up somewhat to a travelled man. A notable personage at these gatherings is Hugh Ferguson, a crabbed-looking little man, past the threescore and ten, and, in some respects, a veritable "character." Hugh has seen a good deal of the world—in fact he has been a wandering sort of individual; and being what is called unsuccessful in life, he is somewhat sour, and disposed to sneer all round. Hugh is comparatively well read, and evidently has been looking into literature of various kinds, useful and otherwise. He is liked, generally speaking, not only for his general information and frequent smart replies, but also because, though not over-wise at times, Hugh is not believed to be of either a violent or a vicious disposition. Ordinarily, in any discussion of importance, the final deliverance rests with Angus Kennedy the blacksmith and Hugh Ferguson the tailor; and by universal consent even the president has occasionally—often, indeed—to yield the palm to Hugh Ferguson.

At the time the Scotch Education Act of 1872 came into operation, frequent and more or less excited conferences anent the matter took place at Angus Kennedy's smithy. The general verdict of these local legislators seemed to be that, while there were "some grawnd raygulayshans" in the new Act, if the schools were getting along as well in other "paireeshes" as in Stratheden, there was little or no need for an altered system. This was pretty much the local sentiment at the date of the passing of the Act. Hugh Ferguson and Angus Kennedy, while agreeing in the main regarding the Act, differed anent the duties of the inspector of schools—Angus strongly insisting that this official should be asked by some competent authority to examine as to the religious instruction. "Na, na, Angus," observed Hugh; "let the parsons look after that business: they hessna owre muckle to do, and they're weel paid for all they do. The inspector canna hev muckle time for asking aboot the long string o' questions aboot 'fectual calling, and original sin, and the likes o' that." "Oh, Hugh, Hugh, take care what you'll be saying!" exclaimed George Morison, brother-in-law of Alexander Mackenzie—one of the elders of the Free Church in Stratheden—from a corner of the smithy, where he had been listening. "It's a lot of people hess need of 'fectual calling, and you shouldna be speakin' that way. Graysheous, whatna lot of strange speaking there's in't in this days aboot 'fectual calling, and questions, and the Bible itself! In my younger days," added George Morison, "it would be only in the church, and at the kattykeesin' (catechising) and prayer-meetings, there would be any speaking aboot them maiters; but now great many will be speaking every place aboot them, and I don't know what's to be in't." The educational question was by this time being lost sight of, the conversation showing — so far, at least, as George Morison was concerned — a tendency to become of a distinctly theological nature. And not seldom is there a theological discussion at the smithy. "I don't know myself what some o' them munnistarrs is aboot; he's an awful man that David Macrae, a munnistarr in the sooth," was the indignant wail of James Maclean, a sour-looking old man, one evening recently at the smithy parliament. "This Macrae," added James, "is saying there's to be no bad place at all, at all, aifter this world! and isn't that awful? They were saying that my own neebour, Sandy Macdougal — daysant good man, he could be an elder any day, but he wouldna take it — they were saying Sandy didna sleep for two nights aifter they told him that a munnistarr was saying there wasna to be a bad place at all — isn't that awful? It was a cruall thing to take the sleep from the hoaly man. But stop you," proceeded our energetic critic — "some people wull know to their cost that there is a bad place! and this David Macrae ——" At this juncture, when, we are grieved to have to suspect, James Maclean was about to relegate the southern parson to regions uninviting, Hugh Ferguson, who was present this evening also, somewhat angrily said to James Maclean, "Haud your tongue, Jeemuss; you're bletherin' aboot what you dinna ken. Are you sure David Macrae is saying there's no to be a bad place, as you call it?" James hesitated before replying to Hugh Ferguson's question: he dreaded it might not be canny to be saying much about such matters in a *mixed* company. At last, however, and as if to vindicate himself, he observed, "Yes; a'm sure he was saying it, because Angus Gordon said he heard Jeemuss Finlayson the deacon saying it, and Jeemuss reads the papers sometimes." At this stage David Grant, a painter in Stratheden, and a native of the parish, who happened to be on business at the smithy on the evening in question, volunteered an observation on the matter. David is an intelligent young man, reads the papers, and has, it is said, a pretty good collection of books of various kinds. " I have been reading about the Rev. David Macrae, and what they're saying against him," observed Grant, "and I don't think he's really saying that at all. It is too great a matter for me to speak about; and more than that, I don't think David Macrae or any other one can make the matter perfectly clear to us. But, James, my friend, yourself nor myself surely cannot see into the like of these matters, but we should all live a good life, and never mind what we cannot see into." "Ah, Maister Grant, we can see weel enough into them fearful munnistarrs that's saying there's to be no bad place." "I scarcely know what your views are, James," added Grant, "but I know very well that my views are like the views of a good lot of the young men of Stratheden. Let us be good men, James, and don't be bothering your head about David Macrae, or any other man. They're all most likely doing their best; and there is One wiser than any of us will decide, and we should leave the matter there." "But surely it's better," said James Maclean, "to have sound views, and to keep to what good men before us said." "But who knows what views are sound?" replied Grant; "every one thinks his own views sound." "Och, Maister Grant, there's the Bible to show it,—to show the richt way," observed James. "All very well, James," replied Grant, "but people don't agree about the Bible. Some say it says this, and others that; but I tell you," added Grant, "the Bible tells us to be good, right living, and honest every way, and there cannot be any doubt about that. We should ask God to help us to be good, James, and leave dark questions." So much for the smithy conferences. They still endure, though not so largely patronised as of old.

The spread of the newspaper, and of cheap literature generally, is diminishing the attendance at these once very popular gatherings.

Prominent among the entertainments of the average Highland parish stands the dancing-school. An institution of this sort periodically appears in Stratheden. Dancing-schools were, and to some extent yet are, especial objects of clerical denunciation in the Highlands. This did, and does, more harm than good. The peaceable members of the community, for the most part trained into dread of the clerical rebuke, even when such rebuke was unwise, kept away from the forbidden entertainment, and it was, as a rule, only such as affected to discard all authority and lived recklessly that became patrons of the unhallowed amusement. Hence, in consequence very much of clerical narrowness and sourness, dancing-schools in Highland parishes long bore a rather uninviting reputation. Matters are much changed to-day. At the same time, though the average resident seems less *afraid* of the dancing-school, it can hardly be said that this institution, so far as the average rural Highland parish is concerned, is always a school of refinement, or a place for acquiring elegant manners and polite conversation.

James Ferguson, a plasterer to trade, and a dancing-master by profession, came to Stratheden last autumn, and announced his intention of opening a dancing-school. Any kind of excitement takes in a place like Stratheden, where novelties are rare, and the dancing-school was the topic of the hour. Alexander Macrae, the old elder, ominously shook his aged head, bewailing the follies of the times; and if he did not pray for those that placed their souls in jeopardy by going to the dancing-school, he was going to do it. So, at least, said Mary Macgillivray, an old maid in Stratheden. She was much of the elder's way of thinking regarding dancing-schools. Mary, however, may have had depressing reflections awakened in her by hearing that so many *young* women attended the dancing-school —young women, that is, with better chances of marriage than herself; and, such is human nature, this may somewhat explain her sympathy with the elder's views. But, and strange to say, another elder of the Free Church, to which church also Alexander Macrae adhered, actually sent three of his family to the dancing-school. Horror seized many of those so-called "good" people at the thought of this shocking declension. The erring elder brought down on his unhappy head, not merely remonstrances for his godless relaxing of parental discipline, but a torrent of wild abuse for the great scandal caused by the enormous iniquity of an *elder* sending his children to a dancing-school. One evening during the currency of the dancing-school a small group happened to meet at one of the Stratheden shops, and, while there, some pupils passed along to the dancing-school. "There they are!" exclaimed Catherine MacKay, a sister of the wife of James Murchison, one of the deacons in the Stratheden Free Church; "a'm afraid they're on the broad way; they'll get plenty room on it for dancing, but a'm thinking it's no dancing that wull be in their heads at the end!" "The dancing will no do them a grain o' ill," replied the young wife of Hugh Kennedy, a mason in Stratheden, "if they'll be decent themselves. It makes people kind o' smart and active like; and ourselves here, though we're as smart and clever like as people in other places, we canna be the worse of getting lessons at the dancing-school." "Ochan! ochan! is that what your sayin'?" retorted Catherine MacKay; "it's easy seen the young people o' this day is gettin' awful strange kind o' views. I think, Mustrass Kennedy, you should go and you'll get a sairman from Hugh MacKay the elder; its awful that he sent his children to the dancing-school. And maybe aifter the sairman, Hugh and yourself—though it wunna be easy for him wi' the lame leg—may hev a reel with the dancing scholars." "Be quate, be quate," exclaimed Angus Matheson, an old, sombre, sour-looking native, of some sixty years of age; "don't be putting sairmans and dancing together that way. If people listened better to sairmans, the dancing wouldn't hev a chance at all. It's awful that people wull go and jump aboot round and round for hours, and they'll be sayin' the sairmans are too long to sit and hear. Ochan! ochan! what are we coming to?" At this stage of the discussion, which was becoming somewhat warm, Thomas Cameron, a respectable tradesman in Stratheden, a man of some five-and-thirty years of age, appeared on the scene; and his shrewd ways and long residence in the south having given him a sort of name in the place, Thomas was at once appealed to for his opinion anent the matter in dispute. "What do you think of this dancing-school that's going on in the paercesh, Maister Cawmurran?" said Catherine MacKay, determined to take a lead in the deliberations, and who would fain get Thomas Cameron to side with her, whatever his own views were. Cameron, taking a practical view of the matter, merely observed that it might be better to wait until the close of the dancing-school to see if any good resulted. The moral or religious aspect of the dispute never entered into Cameron's calculations, so that his cautious, and, as most people will say, wise observation, came rather disappointingly to some of those present. Catherine MacKay, however, determined to have some expression of opinion from Thomas Cameron, remarked, " Don't you think, Maister Cawmurran, the dancing is a sin?" Cameron, slightly irritated at this fanatical view of the matter, replied, "None of your old blether. A sin! there's people winna go to a dancing-school will do far worse." Catherine began to think some strange wild views were beginning to prevail, and she retired from the shop in evident disgust. So much for dancing-schools.

At those seasons when the world generally is supposed to rejoice — Hallowe'en, Christmas, and New Year—Stratheden has its amusements, and they are such as are popular in many Highland parishes of to-day. In most parishes the old style is observed in the three instances specified—namely, November 11th, January 6th, and January 12th. These seasons are not now so generally observed as they were at one time. We remember how, some twenty-five years ago, Hallowe'en was one of the greatest events of the year. Young and old paid homage to the returning season, and the observance included indoor and outdoor amusements. A favourite indoor amusement of those days in some districts of the Highlands was the placing of a silver coin, a ring, or some such valuable, in a preparation of meal and cream, contained in the most capacious basin available in the house, in which preparation some dozen or more spoons eagerly concentrated their energies. Tremendous issues depended on the finding of the ring and coin, and he or she who found either would be soonest married; and a bright future generally, of course, was in store for the successful *spoon*.

The customs of to-day, so far as Hallowe'en, and indeed the other seasons referred to, are concerned, are much the same as at the period indicated, the important difference being that the extent to which they are observed is materially less. The more adventurous give special attention to outdoor amusements. About the middle of autumn it is common in some districts to see schoolboys, when lessons are past, go to the moorland and glens to pluck or cut a sort of long hard grass, some of them bringing home a bundle of about half the size of an ordinary sheaf of corn. This is laid past to dry, and on Hallowe'en used as a torch. When this custom was more largely patronised than now, it was a picturesque sight, on a dark night, to see these youthful torch-light processionists rush along—boys of course rarely walk—the sparkling stream of fire, that spoke of a rapidly fading torch, giving a weird ghastly aspect to the scene, while hearty loud hurrahs were constantly yelled by the happy processionists.

Another Hallowe'en custom of other days yet lingers, and is more extensively honoured than the one just described, though, as will be seen, some people consider it a less harmless amusement. Late at night turnip-fields and kail-gardens are honoured with a visit from some of the fun-loving youths. Nor are these fields and gardens left exactly as they were found: sometimes a considerable number of turnips and cabbages are removed, and, these being distributed among the party, are subsequently disposed of in a manner not a little alarming to some of the quieter inhabitants. Some time during the night the inmates of one or more cottages are startled by a violent crash, as if the door had been smashed in, and this is one of the ways in which some of the turnips are disposed of. Sometimes a door is attacked by a vigorous cannonade of turnips, some 3- and some 5-pounders, all hurriedly but well aimed by the unwelcome nocturnal merrymakers. Another Hallowe'en custom consists in bodily removing a crofter's or "big fairmer's" cart from the steading, and depositing it in some out-of-the-way corner, the search occasionally causing some annoyance and irritation, so carefully is the cart, or plough, or barrow, hid.

All this, generally speaking, is done from harmless motives, though the owners of the turnips and carts, and some others, may have doubts as to the morality of the *amusements* referred to. We have heard it said that any residenter more or less unpopular is sure to receive the larger share of the attentions of Hallowe'en, in the matter of door-hitting and the like. It would be rash, however, to take these attentions as evidence of unpopularity. Most of the merrymaking ones are at a time of life when local strifes, with their envy and hatred, enter but little, if at all, into their deliberations. They hurl the turnips for hurling's sake, and for the fun of it, and that is all.

These customs are on the wane. Somehow they seem to disappear with the remoteness of our Highland parishes, and in consequence of the spread of cheap literature and the increased travelling facilities. It would be foolish to utter a wail over the change. Many of us have happy fond memories of the days when these customs were widely popular, and the average Highlander was then at least as brave, as kindly, and as true as to-day; but seeing the change has brought with it no harm save the sad remembering of those who love to speak of the good old days of long ago, we may composedly accept the altered times.

Of Good Friday, Easter, Candlemas, and even Christmas, little or no notice is taken in the Highlands in the way of practical observance. The New Year, however, is yet observed, though here, too, the custom is diminishing. The old style, as already indicated, is yet observed in Stratheden and in the Highlands generally, but there is a growing feeling in favour of the new style. Many parishes have already adopted the latter, and it must, not long hence, be general. Some of the older natives, of course, adhere rigidly to the old style; and not longer ago than this year of our Lord one thousand eight hundred and eighty, we know of a Highland parish where, while the younger and some of the middle-aged residents observed the new style, the older and more rigid adherents of the old style got up a counter-demonstration on the 12th day of January. With such as observe the New Year, "first-footing" is all the "go" in Stratheden, as in most other places. Before the old year has scarce chimed its last hour, a large proportion of the young men are astir, and each carrying a bottle of mountain-dew, they take their respective ways to neighbours' houses, to exchange the greetings of the season over the contents of the bottle. They sing and laugh and joke after their own fashion, and all are happy, or at least seem to be. Daylight, however, rarely overtakes the hilarity that belongs to an earlier stage of the festivities. At the time when, ordinarily, they get up, many on this day go to bed, exhausted by the wakefulness and walking of the night and morning. Perhaps, too, in one or two instances, something in the nature of a collapse may take place at even an earlier hour than that indicated, as the result, to put it mildly, of a mistaken estimate of their own capacity, or of the power of the mountain-dew, or of both. But we are glad to chronicle there are very few cases of drunkenness; and here we take the opportunity of recording the pleasing fact that the people, generally speaking, are essentially temperate in the use of intoxicating drink. In the early New Year morning some few persons— those that wisely accepted the blessed gift of sleep, or prudently maintained a wakeful coolness the whole livelong night—may be seen careering along the hillsides and straths, bound for some neighbour's cottage, singing a festive song with voices seemingly not yet subdued by serious contact with the cares of life. It is not the silly maudlin song that comes of intoxication, but, as a rule, the genuine outburst of a young and gladsome heart. As the day advances, groups, of two or three or more, family and other groups, may be seen passing along to exchange neighbourly greetings. In some houses there is at night a substantial *tea* spread, to which a few neighbours are invited. There is a return tea next evening in another house, so that the New Year festivities are thus often prolonged for a week. This return feasting is much in vogue, and on such occasions, tables that sometimes are bare enough, literally groan under the heavy variety of eatables and drinkables. A very remarkable feature of such entertainments lately came under our notice. A resident in a parish not fifty miles from Stratheden, in speaking of such matters, strong in the belief—a pretty common one—that a hugely laden table on such occasions is very essential, observed with a look of pride, referring to the parish he lives in, "Plenty of oor people kill *half* a pig at the New Year!" Here, surely, is a case for the anti-vivisectionists. It would not apparently be easy, if, indeed, it would be possible, to find a clearer case of vivisection.

Card-playing (no betting as a rule) is yet a somewhat popular amusement in the Highlands, and many a long winter evening it helps to while away. Some of the older natives look on card-playing as altogether an unsanctified matter, and plainly enough express their belief that it is a practice specially under the direction of the foe of all good. Some of these people have a superstitious dread of the mere sight of cards, and shudder at the silent, harmless stare of the knave of clubs, more than, probably, they would at the club of a knave, or even a Zulu's assegai. Not many days ago, one of the Stratheden people—a person believing card-playing to be "no richt"—gravely told us that at a house in the neighbourhood of Stratheden, where a game at cards was being played, "something awful took place for to make them give it up." Our informant alleged that in the case in question the cards indulged in a spiritualistic dance on their own account, — some leaping to the roof, some taking a suicidal plunge into the fire, and a remnant mysteriously disappearing beneath the table on which, but a few moments before, they quietly lay. Card-playing, however, yet endures. Farmhouse kitchens, and shoemakers' and tailors' shops, are the favourite rendezvous of card-players. Happily, strong drink is as rare at these gatherings as is the practice of betting; but the conversation accompanying card-playing is not always edifying.

The telling of ghost-stories may be classed among the popular entertainments. This was at one time a very popular practice in the family circle and at *ceilidh* gatherings; but the railway train has whistled many a ghost out of existence, and consequently materially curtailed the number of ghost-stories. The newspaper and the travelling facilities, also, have recently been very successfully attacking the ghost and ghost-story strongholds. But even to-day this once very common practice is to some extent observed. The haunted localities laid under contribution include places out of and in "the paereesh." When the alleged haunted locality is near at hand, there is, of course, a more anxious look towards the door, and a closer creeping near the fireplace, among, at least, the younger members of the listening group. Even to-day some Stratheden people gravely allege that "uncanny" lights and unearthly yells frequent a *wood* in the parish. If, by way of accounting for the lights, tinkers' tents are mentioned, the reply is, "Och no, indeed; it's far worse nor tinkers that's in't. You'll see they'll be something yet where the light waas." If a howl of a wandering dog be suggested as explanatory of the yell, the reply sometimes is, "Och, indeet, it's no that kind o' noise —people knows what's in't, and that it's no a right noise; but there will be something come oot o' that noise yet."

In speaking to a Stratheden man the other day on the subject of ghosts, we took occasion to notice that the railway, and the constant moving about of the people, in addition to other agencies, must have scared away the ghosts, if ever there were any. "Ochan! ochan! sir," he replied, "it's no a train or anything o' that kind that can put away the ghosts. What do *they* care for trains and *that?* They're saying" (and this story was believed by not a few in Stratheden) "that last Sawbath night, when the train was coming near Stratheden, a big, big black thing stopped it and it couldna go, and they tried and tried, and it wouldna go. The *object* wouldna move, nor speak, nor anything. Now, Maister Mackenzie," he added, "*that* waas a ghost; and it's no right for trains to be going on the Sawbath."

Some readers by this time may be asking, what about the *musical* entertainments? Does not this element continue to occupy a prominent place in the popular entertainments of a Highland parish?

What about Gaelic songs? Surely Stratheden is rich in the department of Gaelic song-singing? Are not Ossian's strains familiar sounds? Are not the plaintive melodies of the bards, of Rob Donn, of M'Intyre, and others, often sung in the family circle and at festive gatherings? Do not the young maidens of the parish often sing love-songs in the Gaelic tongue?

Much though many will regret it, these questions, so far as the average Highland parish of to-day is concerned, must severally be answered in the negative. As to concerts, we have already indicated the measure of popularity they enjoy in some parishes. Songs are sung, of course; but in comparison with even fifteen years ago, the proportion sung in Gaelic is small indeed. Even Ossian, though revered by Highlanders generally, is read by few; and there are many to-day to whom Ossian's classic page is very much of a foreign tongue. Mackay (Rob Donn), M'Intyre, and various other Gaelic bards, are spoken of; but their songs, though found in most cottages affecting anything like a library, are rarely sung. Such of the young maidens as are given to singing, in the great majority of cases, find expression for their tender emotions in the English language. Gaelic songs are to-day oftener heard in Glasgow, Edinburgh, and Aberdeen, than in many Highland parishes; and those Highlanders that in these and other distant places sing the fondly cherished melodies of long ago, — melodies that awaken fond though mingled memories of the old home "in the misty island" or the distant glen,— will doubtless feel disposed to sigh over what many of them no doubt will consider the melancholy declension in the matter of Gaelic song-singing in Highland parishes.

In the department of purely literary entertainment, Stratheden has not much to boast of. Efforts have recently been made to establish a society, professedly having in view, by means of essays, lectures, and debates, the cultivating of literary tastes, and, generally, the mental improvement of the members; but it remains to be seen what good, if any, it will accomplish in the way of promoting reading habits, a manly toleration in matters of Church and creed, and general intelligence. In too many Highland parishes such societies, though making a promising beginning, soon exhibit signs of an approaching collapse. This is not owing to the inexperience of the members, or to the fact that some of the essays are dull, and some of the debates stupid and ludicrously conducted. There is many a literary society, now flourishing, that experienced similar early disadvantages. The great barrier to the genuine progress of such a society consists, in some places, in the fact that the old miserable leaven of sectarianism finds its way into its counsels. The society is started ostensibly on an unsectarian basis, but too often this is but a pretext to secure *public* countenance. In course of time sectarian animosities, descending at times to venomous and cowardly personalities, are ventilated; but it is right to add that such contemptible displays, as a rule, come from the adherents of the ecclesiastical sect that is numerically the stronger in the Highlands, and that the unhopeful feelings alluded to are kept alive and promoted chiefly by those who should be the first to endeavour to scare them away.

At this stage we fancy we hear some enthusiastic admirer of the *ideal* Highland parish wonderingly ask, what about the *bagpipes?* Have the strains of this ancient instrument, that used to speak to Highland hearts and stir the Highland blood, been swamped in the newer noises of the changes of to-day? By no means; and it is only because it is not now so much, so to speak, the universal musical instrument, that we have delayed reference to it. There are some changes that will be variously viewed, but most of us would consider a Highland parish sadly forfeiting its claim to interest and regard — sadly adrift, indeed, from what a Highland parish should be—if within it were unknown the stirring strains of the ancient bagpipes. Some of the young lads of Stratheden play them, and not seldom from a cottage here and there one may hear "the pibroch sounding deep over mountain and glen." These amateur players, when asked, give their services willingly at weddings, balls, and harvest-homes; but it is in his home, to the delight of his brothers and sisters, though not, in every case, quite to the delight of the older people, some of whom have a pharisaic horror of all secular, and especially of instrumental, music, that the amateur chiefly plays. There are other musical instruments coming into general use, such as concertinas and accordions; nor are the notes of the violin unknown. While, however, it will be a long time before any, or even all of these, will succeed in swamping the strains of the ancient bagpipes, we are glad to think it will be longer still before the narrow-minded and pharisaic fanatics of the community will be able to put to silence any one of these instruments, all of which, when sorrow comes, or time hangs wearily, are capable of affording much comfort and bettering entertainment.

CHAPTER VIII.

SHOPKEEPING IN A HIGHLAND PARISH OF TO-DAY.

BEFORE railway and steamboat communication became widely developed in the Northern Highlands —up till about twenty years ago—shopkeeping in the average Highland parish was rather a good business. The carrier—whose cart, as a rule, was of very limited dimensions—the sailing sloop, the small coasting steamer, and the coach, supplied the ordinary means of importing goods; and the facilities thus afforded left but a scant margin for competition in each district. The commercial traveller was comparatively unknown, and local competition was slight indeed. As a rule, there was but one or at most two substantial shops in each Highland parish of those days; and the *merchant*, with which designation the shopkeeper is almost invariably dignified by the native residents of a Highland parish, had the field almost entirely to himself. He was a general dealer, and sold tea, sugar, coffee, cloth, bonnets, ribbons, pots and pans, treacle, salt, tobacco, pepper, mouse and rat traps, fishing-hooks, eyes for other hooks, and these latter hooks themselves, and various other articles literally too numerous to mention. He was able at all times to meet the ordinary local wants. He might not, and did not, feel any great alarm at the rumours periodically circulated that some one intended starting an opposition shop; and yet he did not feel absolutely secure in his monopoly, for the increasing travelling facilities introduced the commercial traveller, and the merchant of the period we speak of indicated no strong wish to cultivate the acquaintance of the "trayvullar." The latter might encourage, might actually set agoing, competition, and as for his own supply of "goods," the merchant himself could go to "Glessga" twice a-year for that purpose; so that really, so thought the merchant, "the trayvullar micht stay at hoam."

But the growing facilities of communication gradually began to modify the supremacy and curtail the trade of the merchant, who, hitherto, had matters very much his own way. By the aid of large and powerful steamers, and the extension of railway communication, our remotest Highland parishes were soon brought within comparatively easy access of the great centres of commerce. Commercial travellers, representing retail as well as wholesale houses, now frequently visit every nook and corner of the Highlands. Not only do these travellers transact business with the shopkeepers, but those of them that represent retail houses take orders directly from the native and other residents. In this way a new, and, from the local shopkeeper's point of view, a less promising, era began to dawn in the commercial sky of the Northern Highlands.

Nor was the competition confined to that caused by the frequent visits of commercial travellers, and the growing facilities for getting "goods" direct from the south. There are other competing agencies that, very much in consequence of the facilities alluded to, soon appeared on the scene, and some of them, to this day, receive no small patronage. There is the packman, with his ready-made men's clothes, handkerchiefs, collars, and neckties; and there is the packwoman, endeavouring in like manner to meet the female requirements in dress and other commodities. Then there is the travelling merchant, who calls himself a jeweller, carrying a box containing a very varied assortment of watches, chains, knives and forks, thimbles, pins, hooks and eyes, and needles,—all which articles are, as a rule, far higher in price than in value. For a long time these peripatetic vendors succeeded in driving a flourishing trade. In the days when the average native had little capacity or inclination for scanning certain features of the packman's commercial creed, the latter and others of a similar calling contrived to make it a matter of established belief that a transaction with them meant a bargain—and hence very much their success. The growing habit among families, however, of getting goods direct from Inverness, Aberdeen, Edinburgh, and Glasgow, which goes so far to curtail the trade of the local shopkeeper, must, and does, very materially interfere with the success of the travelling vendor's trade.

Within recent years an additional opposition to local shopkeeping enterprise has made its presence known, in the shape of what may be called a travelling bazaar. This institution visits many of our Highland parishes twice yearly. Ordinarily three or four persons conduct the "business." They come by train with large boxes and hampers containing a great variety of goods, such as clocks, looking-glasses, pen-knives, spectacles, watch-chains, knives and forks, purses, pocket-books, combs, and brushes. They transact business in somewhat of the lottery fashion, and by their haranguing and their manner of displaying the commodities for sale, make elaborate and often ridiculous efforts to impress the residents with a sense of the marvellous bargains to be had — of the unparalleled cheapness of the "goods." Large bills are posted on prominent places announcing the arrival of this institution of marvellous bargains; and the bazaar, so well do the elaborate and even the ridiculous efforts succeed, is literally crowded during the two or three evenings it remains open. It is proper to observe, as a reason why the various institutions spoken of constitute opposition to the local shopkeepers, that the various commodities sold by the former are, as a rule, sold by the latter.

And yet, strange to say, shopkeeping seems to flourish in Highland parishes. With all the competition specified—and it is growing where it is most powerful—the noteworthy fact remains, that within recent years the number of local shops has been increasing. In Stratheden there are to-day over a dozen shops; and twenty years ago, when the population was larger than to-day, there were only two, while some few years previously one shop did duty for the whole parish. And how is this rather remarkable phenomenon to be explained? It is just because, as a Stratheden shopkeeper remarked to us a few days ago, there is a belief prevalent in the community that shopkeeping is a sure and an easy way of making money. Some native and other residents see the shopkeeper, his wife, and bairns, donning the "grawndest kind o' clothes in the paereesh," and, with a strong faith in appearances, the wondering observers conclude the shop must be something of a veritable mint. " Why toil," say some of these wondering ones, " when a shop, which brings in money so quickly and with so little trouble, may be so easily put up ?" It is very much in consequence of such short-sighted reflections and rash conclusions that so remarkable an increase in the number of local shops has taken place within recent years. A crofter's son goes south, lays by a few pounds of money, returns to his native parish on the decease of his father, to take possession of the croft, and gets himself established in the old home. He is not long at home until he thinks the few pounds he has managed to save cannot be more profitably employed than in the purchase of some groceries and the other usual equipments of a Highland shop, and he launches on a commercial undertaking. A crofter dies, and his widow, preferring to give up the croft, converts the stock of the croft into money, by means of which a shop is started, and hence another addition to the local commercial establishments. George, son of Angus Morison, a Stratheden crofter, went to Glasgow some ten years ago, and though his ambition soared no higher than that of being a "hand" on board one of the Clyde dredgers, he managed to save some little money. A kind of home-feeling, which certain shrewd ones say is akin to laziness, seized George, and coming back to his home in Stratheden, he started a shop in a small wooden shed at the end of his father's house. Old William Nicolson, a Stratheden crofter, died, leaving a widow and an only daughter, the latter called Janet. There was a small apartment on the premises, in which the father, who was somewhat of a carpenter, used to work whenever the requirements of the croft admitted. It was now unused, and Janet Nicolson and her mother came to think that it might be profitably occupied. Why not buy some pounds of tea, a hundredweight or two of sugar, and some other commodities, and start a shop? And these two did start a shop. Nor was the strictly commercial aspect of the venture the sole ambition. By the opening of the shop, a twofold object is gained. The unused carpenter's room again becomes useful, and—so at least think herself and her mother—Janet's *matrimonial* prospects are improved. Might not one or other of the Stratheden young lads, who do not by any means despise money or a croft, nor for that matter a shop, consider Janet, whatever her former and other charms, doubly attractive *in* or *with* the shop? What although certain ones in the parish—envious young women, disappointed mothers, and, it may be, rejected suitors — might say all sorts of malicious things whenever Janet's approaching marriage is announced? Events of this nature, of course, are freely commented on, especially in rural districts, and it is scarcely to be expected that all the observations made will be unprejudiced. The wife and daughter of Alexander Maclean, a Stratheden crofter, " from the first "—as they said—and, ostensibly, in no degree influenced by the news of the coming marriage, considered it foolish, if not daring and utterly reckless, of the aforesaid Janet and her mother to start a shop. "What were *they* going to do wi' a shop?" observed Mrs Alexander Maclean—"there's plenty o' shops before; and Jennat Neeculsan wi' her pride, and tryin' to be grawnd and *that*, you'll see she will soon *broke*, and what will the grawnd shop do then? It wud look more liker her, the hussy, to work wi' a spade on the lawnd nor a shop." But

Alexander Maclean's wife and daughter have no money—no possible means, indeed, of starting a shop, however much inclined—so that it is perfectly unnecessary narrowly to scan the motive under which these two critics gave their verdict anent "Jennat Neeculsan's" mercantile undertaking.

Some of the shops thus suddenly appearing, as suddenly vanish from the scene—an announcement for which, doubtless, the reader is well prepared. It is consoling to think, however, that beyond the few pounds embarked in the too rash venture, no serious loss accrues, and that some of these adventurous would-be shopkeepers restore their undivided attention to their crofts, or other occupation, wiser, if not richer people.

There are in Stratheden, as already mentioned, over a dozen shops — but, with three exceptions, they are very small and unassuming institutions. In almost every instance the shopkeeper has a croft, and in more than half the cases the shop is a mere accessory of the croft. The shopkeepers, without exception, do what is called a *general* business or trade. Parcels of drapery fill one shelf, biscuit-boxes another, and a mongrel collection of confections, nails, thread, buttons, needles and pins, a third. The universal tea-chest adorns one corner, and the accompanying sugar-barrel another; while, in addition to a host of other commodities, metal pots and pans and other kitchen utensils are suspended along the shelves in a way not particularly complimentary to the shopkeeper's idea of harmony or arrangement. A few of the shops, as has been indicated, are of a very unpretending character—so far as both edifice and merchandise are concerned, and in such instances no "sign" adorns the building to tell the passer-by or would-be customer what commodities are for sale, or that any are for sale. Such establishments, however, must soon disappear. Larger shops than those that in other days were found sufficient to meet the local requirements in the average Highland parish are making their appearance, and these must of necessity soon swamp the smaller fry.

There is one shop in Stratheden very much larger than the largest of the others, and its existence is another proof of the contrast the Stratheden of to-day presents to the Stratheden of even fifteen years ago. In most respects this shop eclipses the smaller establishments that used to do duty before the *ceannaiche mor* (big merchant) opened what some of the native residents, proud of local enterprise, admiringly call the "big warehoose." The other shops in Stratheden have two elements in common—scanty light and limited space; but the "big warehoose," built in 1879, is well lighted and roomy. The windows, relatively speaking, are of immense capacity—the panes indeed being, according to the local idea, so large that some of the older natives, credulous, and yet doubtful, for a long time hesitated to believe that there were panes at all! Another sign of progress is observable in the almost elaborate advertising displays and other decorations with which the said windows are done up by the "big merchant." The new shop is also roomy enough—not merely in the space devoted to the "goods," but as well in the space ordinarily allotted to customers. This latter is an important fact in such a place as Stratheden, where customers are not, as a rule, in a great hurry in making their purchases, and where it is usual to make the shop a place of concourse for gossip, sometimes harmless, but not seldom low and despicable. This latter custom, however, like the kindred one of going to *ceilidh* in neighbours' houses, is on the wane; but those that yet respect the habit will warmly appreciate the roomy feature of the "big warehoose." The "big merchant" is a man of some enterprise, and, indeed, is somewhat

of a credit to Stratheden—his native parish. The
son of a crofter, he left home for the south in early
life, and pursued his trade of house-carpenter, making some little money by his industry and prudent
economy. Returning to Stratheden, he opened a
small shop; but finding his trade increasing, he
resolved to build a large shop, and hence the "big
warehoose." Ronald Macgregor—the big merchant
—is a shrewd, sensible sort of individual. Not only
was he his own architect in planning and carrying
on the building of the house—a substantial, neat-looking modern cottage—but he himself wrought
most of the carpenter-work. And not only so;
the furniture — chairs, sofas, tables, and basin-stands—have been made by Ronald; and these
articles of furniture would bear favourable comparison with some articles in the more elaborate
displays of some city cabinetmakers' and upholsterers' galleries. Certain of the wiseacres of the
parish—who knows but some of the occupants of
the smaller shops are of the number?—have been
freely commenting on what they call the folly of
having built so large a structure and opened so
large a shop in a place where there were so many
shops before. Be this as it may, the building and
the shop are there; and whatever be the success

SHOPKEEPING IN A HIGHLAND PARISH. 193

of the shop, it seems likely it will work in the direction of absorbing some of the smaller commercial establishments.

It is a noteworthy fact, that the ancient custom of "barter" to this day holds in many Highland parishes. It is daily honoured in the shopkeeping ways of Stratheden. The tea-loving matron, whose live stock consists of a dozen or so of barn-door fowls, will go to a shopkeeper with a dozen of eggs, and get in exchange an ounce of tea, a small package of sugar, and a few biscuits. The barter transaction is not seldom of a very unpretending kind. Not many days ago we saw a little girl enter a shop in the parish with a couple of eggs, and get in return for these two eggs "a heppany's worth o' washin'-soda and a heppany's worth o' pins." Nor are eggs the only commodity offered in barter. Butter, potatoes, and wool do duty in perpetuating this lingering custom; and a week or two ago we were told of a rather special case of barter that occurred in Stratheden a few days previously, where a cart was exchanged for a sheep and a pig!

Some of the natives—those especially that have travelled but little—have a high estimate of the importance of the local shops. We know of an incident that at once illustrates this consciousness of local importance, and that shows how vague the ideas are that are prevalent among some people in the far North regarding the size of such places as Glasgow. A few years ago a Highland shopkeeper went to Glasgow to bring home the half-yearly supply of "goods." Among those at the shop on the day of his return was his father, an aged man who had never been much away from the remote solitudes and the simple ways of his native parish. As the goods—an assortment of the usual belongings of a Highland shop, and worth, in the aggregate, about £60 — lay at the shop-door, the amazed father, proud no doubt that so many of the neighbours were seeing what he considered the enterprise and importance of his son, observed—" Cha'n fheumadh Glaschu gum biodh mo mhacsa dol tric ann" (Glasgow could ill afford that my son would go there often)! The poor old man evidently thought that, if his son made many such demands on the resources of Glasgow, it would be time to consider whether the city could really continue to "flourish"!

It must be confessed that, in ordering "goods," a rather peculiar specimen of letter-writing occasionally finds its way from the Highland shopkeeper to the "Glessga merchant." As is the case in other places, and with some other people, the shopkeeper is not always at home either in grammar or spelling; nor indeed is his English always clear. An old shopkeeper in the West Highlands, it is said, in ordering a quantity of shoe-tacks, put the order in this form: "Wull you be so goot and for to sent me a *mile* of tacks." The number of tacks he wanted was one thousand, and the Gaelic for a thousand and for a mile sounds the same. And even in the matter of addressing letters, persons of this description have been known to display some rather amusing eccentricities. Not many years ago a Highland shopkeeper, in writing to the master of a small coasting-sloop, made a somewhat remarkable addition to the address. It had been arranged that the shopkeeper was to write the captain of the sloop to some port at which the latter was to call, and "to be kept till called for" was to be added to the address. The shopkeeper adopted an independent plan of indicating the direction agreed upon, and addressed the letter thus :—

"*Capteen Funla Cawmurran*,
Slup Jeen and Mary,
Glenellag,
Proatford,
Skye.
And stop there"!

Shopkeeping in Stratheden and like places is not ordinarily a toilsome occupation. The principal transactions take place in the forenoon and late in the evening. It is probably owing to the procrastinating tendency prevalent in other places than Highland parishes that so many seem to find a peculiar fascination in going to the shop at, or very near, closing-time. The practice, of course, lightens the duties of the day, so far as the shopkeeper is concerned, but unnecessarily prolongs the late hours that form a common feature in the shopkeeping, or rather the shopping, in at least the more rural of Highland parishes. No doubt for a large portion of the year the croft duties, in the case of many customers, occasion late shopping, and this may suit the shopkeeper well enough too; for, in several cases, he likewise has his croft, and it might be irritating enough, even to the greediest of shopkeepers, to be called from the field on a fine harvest-day, in uncertain weather, to sell "a heppany's worth o' washin'-soda," or even to give an ounce of tea in exchange for half-a-dozen eggs.

In the case of the shopkeeper that has no croft, the time, as a rule, passes wearily. Ordinarily, he is not what one would call a great reader, though he considers himself, as some others do, "acquent with lots o' maiters, and a persan o' eddikayshan." He, of course, gets his newspaper—is not seldom, indeed, a local news-agent—and his reputation as an "authority" might suffer did he not keep himself posted up, in a kind of way, in "what the papers are saying." He does not, however, spend much time over his paper. He soon reads all he feels an interest in—all, perhaps, that he can understand; and, inasmuch as his shop duties do not ordinarily occupy much time, his life, generally speaking, is idle beyond dispute. In rural districts, where there is so much stillness, and where so many have little to do, there is a strong curiosity to see what is going on around, who is on the move, and the phenomenon of a stranger often excites this curiosity to a very high pitch indeed. The shopkeeper largely shares in this peculiarity. He has plenty of time, and has at least as much interest as any other person in the local movements —and a stranger is a possible customer.

In not a few cases the shopkeeper is considered by some in the parish to be a veritable "authority." It is on local matters especially that he is considered so; and very probably he owes his investiture with this character in a great measure to the fact that his position enables him to hear most of the local gossip. News of most things that happen in "the paereesh," and, of course, news of things that never happen, seem to gravitate rapidly towards the shop as the central local news-office. "They're saying this," and "they're saying that," are ordinarily the prefaces to the bits of news circulated in such places, and no one is hungrier than the merchant to hear what "they're saying." He can tell others, and these will inspire third parties with a wish to visit the shop to hear what "they're saying," and somehow it may help the trade of the shop. The shopkeeper at least seems to think so, and accordingly countenances—nay, strongly encourages—the news-vending practice. He invariably assumes the bearing of an utterly impartial listener of the shop gossip. In fact nothing else would pay; for unfriendly comments are, of course, sometimes made on absent customers, and these latter would soon hear if "the merchant" said anything unkind about them.

Archibald Morison is one of the principal shopkeepers in Stratheden, and a good representative of the fraternity. He is a man of some sixty years of age, and, though not a native, is somewhat popular—more so, indeed, than those whom some of the people call *strenjars* usually are. His shop, which occupies a central position in the parish, is often largely frequented—not, however, so much by customers as by loungers and gossips—and contains the usual varied commodities already referred to. Archy possesses somewhat of what is called the "gift of the gab," and is considered smart by the sort of people that usually visit his shop on business, or for hearing what "they're saying." Some of his so-called smart sayings are weak, and some indeed are vulgar—coarse, perhaps; but then, as in all other places, some of the frequenters of his shop are weak, some vulgar, and a few, it may be, are coarse. Archy, no doubt, is a decent enough sort of fellow as the world goes, being, indeed, of a kindly disposition, and, comparatively speaking, liberal-minded, while many of his customers are intelligent and highly respectable people; but other types of humanity, of course, frequent Archy's shop, so that he must try to be "a'body's body," and have a word for all.

The character of the conversations usually taking place at Archibald Morison's shop is mixed, and, as a rule, unedifying and profitless rather than otherwise. Such questions and comments as the following are often heard: "Was it at Sandy Macgregor the munnistarr *waas* last Sawbath? Loash! didna he get it fearfell? Sandy shouldna be running away to that Moaderat church whatever; am sure, though there wasna preachin' in oor own church, people shouldna be wantering to the Moaderats. Loash, try wull Sandy go again! Messtur Neeculsan was nearly mat aboot it. Ach, Messtur Neeculsan can speak strong—it's hum that can; and he's a quate lad, though he was speaking so angry agenst the Moaderats; but it's no easy for hum to be seeing his people wantering to some places. Och, no indeet." Such is a specimen of the ecclesiastical comments ordinarily ventilated in Archy's shop. The ecclesiastical, however, form but a portion of the observations usually advanced. National politics receive a kind of attention, and petty local prejudices and paltry personalities are too often ventilated. The political observations sometimes take the following shape: "They're battlin' terrable in Parlimant aboot wars, and Soloos, and black lads, and places far away *foreign*, and *that;* it would be wiserlike o' them to send us the tobawca and the tea chape, and send a lot o' the money to the poor man." Local prejudices manifest themselves in such expressions as: "Mercy me! isna Donald Ferragussan's wife a nessty hussy wi' her silks? It would be better for her to send a grainy o' meal to her ould father and the rest o' her poor freends." Another says, "Did you hear of the awful quarrall atween the wife o' Angus Maclean, the shuppard, and the wife o' William Fraser, the plaisturrar? Angus's wife was sayin' fearfell things aboot William Fraser—that he's a nessty man, though he's so foand o' speakin' aboot releejan and goin' to meetins; and, indeed, myself thinks she wassna far wrong. William's a very wicked man, and he shouldna be askin' the 'croft' that my father was in." These must suffice as specimens of the shop conversations, and we gladly pass from them in the hope that a growing culture and a more edifying use of time will elevate the character of at least some of the sentiments now too often uttered in such places.

Such, generally speaking, is shopkeeping in the average Highland parish of to-day. One of the principal elements in the changes of to-day—the increased facilities of communication with the centres of commerce—has greatly modified its character; and this influence will very probably continue to be even more powerfully felt, and that chiefly in the direction of removing what even the natives themselves now call "the wee bits o' shoppies" to the domain of an unreturning past.

CHAPTER IX.

THE HOME AND SURROUNDINGS OF A "BIG FAIRMER" IN A HIGHLAND PARISH OF TO-DAY.

BURNSIDE COTTAGE, the residence of Mr Malcolm Macgregor—one of the principal farmers in Stratheden—is a snug-looking edifice situated at the foot of a picturesque hill. It is a comparatively modern structure, and, in point of design and accommodation, is far in advance of the kind of habitation in which lived the great majority of Highland farmers some forty years ago. The situation and surroundings are essentially picturesque. The cottage nestles cosily in a nook, sheltered, in Nature's own inimitable fashion, by the majestic hills that encircle the spot. On one side, a little distance away, there rises a massive oval-shaped hill, and for some considerable distance up the slope of this hill there is a wood, which, when decked in the variegated autumn tints, forms a pretty contrast to the rugged, rocky hills around. Quite near, there runs a river fed by numerous streamlets from the neighbouring hills; and when water is abundant — which will happen, though the climate of Stratheden is not a moist one — a waterfall, only a few yards away from Burnside Cottage, beats its weird and not unmusical time on the gurgling waters in the river's bed. Looking eastward, from an eminence quite near the cottage, a very fine picture of natural scenery presents itself. For some distance along there is a considerable extent of cultivated ground, circular in shape, a broad stream with miniature islands forming the diameter, and rocky, heathery hills standing out in bold relief on either side. Farther on, in the same direction, patches of richest green are visible in the distant valley; while, a little way beyond, the eye catches sight of the far-off sea stretching far away, until it and the horizon seem to meet and vanish out of sight. And those that love the music of the voice, as well as Nature's silent grandeur, may find, amid the scene here described, much to delight the ear and speak to the heart. There is a clump of trees right opposite Burnside Cottage in which the winged songsters seem to love to warble, and we have often listened with delight to their cheering concert. The mavis and the lark, — the latter has not yet disappeared from Stratheden,—often pipe their sweet song in or near that clump of trees; and if the lapwing sometimes sweeps along with its not inviting music, the contrast but makes the listener the better prize the happy music of the smaller birds. The milkmaid's song, too, in the still summer evening echoes along the neighbouring rocks "when the kye come hame," and an occasional low from "crummie" herself echoes far down the Strath — and this latter, though not always a sound remarkable for melody, is sufficiently in keeping with the surroundings to constitute an additional charm; while, as if responding, there strike upon the ear, with a pleasing music of their own, the lowing of other "crummies" browsing on the hillsides, and the bleating of sheep feeding in the distant glen.

Mr Malcolm Macgregor, as the natives generally say, is a "big fairmer," and owns some three thousand sheep. His stock is composed chiefly of Cheviots, or *caoraich mhor* (big sheep), as the Gaelic-speaking residents call them, in contradistinction to the *caoraich bheag* (little sheep), or black-faced—which latter kind formed the bulk of the stock of sheep-holders generally in Highland parishes before the days of the modern "big fairmer." Malcolm Macgregor is a good specimen of the better class of farmers in the Highlands of to-day. He has a thoroughly practical knowledge of his profession—which, of course, is necessary for successful farming in the Highlands, as in every other place—and when occasion requires, he does not consider it beneath his dignity to take a share of the manual work of the farm. From his youth he has been familiar with sheep-farming— his father, a genuine Highlander, and a shrewd industrious man, being a farmer occupying extensive sheep-holdings; and the son seems to have inherited some of the shrewdness and perseverance of the father.

Macgregor is a man of great despatch—so much so, indeed, that some might think that at times he is even too hurried, too anxiously eager; but it is his way, and that, we suppose, is the philosophy of such individual features. We have heard, however, some farmers say that certain ones in Malcolm's profession in Highland and other parishes might be the better of a little of the said despatch; that some "big fairmers" show too much of a proneness to the easy-going style of life— seeming imperturbably satisfied, so to speak, with the *status quo* idea, and having apparently unlimited faith in the usual returns, prices, and the like. Be this as it may, and merely observing that increasing competition must tend to diminish the number of easy-going farmers, we proceed to observe that, with Malcolm Macgregor, farming is not an amusement merely. He looks on it as a real, and, as many others in these days of foreign competition and severe seasons will think, a very arduous profession, and wisely concludes that it is the duty of every farmer to leave no proper effort untried towards making the farm pay. Macgregor's ideas of farming, however, are not altogether confined by considerations as to what will pay. The æsthetic element enters somewhat into his musings regarding the management of his farm. He is strong in improving tendencies, as some other Highland farmers of to-day are, and might become a successful and even famous land-reclaimer were his energies entirely devoted in this direction. In the few years he has been in Burnside, he has made considerable alterations with the view of beautifying the immediate surroundings of his home. The cottage itself was all that could be desired — commodious and compact, and is such, indeed, as the most fastidious farmer might be pleased with; but Macgregor thought there was room for improvement in the immediate surroundings. The lawn in front was pretty enough, but it looked bare, and the planting of trees and shrubs was resolved on.

The ordinary daily life of a "big fairmer" in a Highland parish does not abound in events of specially exciting interest. Lambing time, clipping time, the big wool-market days, smearing time, and a few busy days in spring and harvest, constitute the principal events in his calendar. District shows, also, of cattle, sheep, and farm-produce, occasion some slight ripple on the comparatively unmoved sea of the average Highland farmer's life. There is always, no doubt, plenty of room for activity and diligence, and, nowadays especially, no small need for the exercise of both; nor will any rightthinking person fail to sympathise with farmers in the difficulties they have, as a class, to contend against in these unmistakably changed days of farming in Scotland generally.

Highland farmers and their families, in their tastes and general ways, present somewhat of a contrast to those of about forty years ago. The simpler tastes and primitive ways of the days of yore are rapidly disappearing. The style of living in diet, dress, and general home surroundings, has much changed within even the last twenty years—the tendency being, it need hardly be added, towards more luxurious and expensive ways. In the matter of diet, perhaps, the change is not so marked, if we except the now more common use of those table delicacies—such as desserts and fruit accompaniments—which every farmer's wife in all Highland parishes of to-day endeavours to command, especially when there are strangers staying at the house, or even temporarily dining there. With regard to dress, except in some far-away secluded spot, where remnants of older fashions yet are honoured, the homespun and like humble fabrics worn by most of the Highland farmers of some forty and even twenty-five years ago are all but unknown; and as for the lady members of the farmer's family, it is hardly necessary to say that by them the latter form of progress is especially patronised.

With the more elaborate architectural design now shown by farmers' houses, a grander, more costly style of furniture has, of course, come to be used.

And there are other evidences of the changed times. The sons and daughters of the farmer of to-day are supposed to get a more fashionable or more "finished" education than was common among the same class at the period alluded to. Libraries in farmers' houses, also, are more elaborate than of yore; but this does not mean in every case a greater cultivation of reading habits. There were, as many know, at the time referred to, as cultured and well-read farmers as the most cultured of to-day; and indeed we are not sure but that there was a broader, healthier refinement in some instances then than is now ordinarily met with, even among the better class of Highland farmers. Farmers, very probably, as a class, are better educated to-day; and there is no reason why they should not be so, seeing their advantages are so much greater. But some farmers and their families, just like other people, in their manner of speaking, and in their style of commenting on persons they envy or dislike, afford quite ample evidence that more than education so called—more than grandeur in dress and equipage, and costliness in diet—is needed for the encouragement of that cultured, generous refinement which bespeaks the lady and the gentleman.

Altogether the simpler ways of other times, generally speaking, are gone, though it is not easy to admit that the change is, in every instance, an unmixed good. If, as a class, farmers' wives are to-day better read and more accomplished generally, we have met with certain shrewd ones—farmers too, men able to compare both periods—who allege that, whatever be the progress of our time, there are among the farmers' wives of the present day more industrious gossips and busybodies in other people's matters than of yore. To what extent the allegation is well founded we need not inquire, and will merely add that we like to think that any farmers' wives that do give way to the too common weaknesses of excessive gossip and busybodyism, form the exceptions among a highly respectable and kindly class of persons.

Some may think that there are other unpromising features associated with the so-called advanced circumstances of the Highland farmers of to-day,—so far, that is to say, as some of them are concerned. Many of us have heard, longer ago than we care to think of, that "all work and no play makes Jack a dull boy;" but if the converse be true, some farmers in some Highland parishes of to-day should be the very opposite of dull. With such it is all play and no work, and it is unnecessary to say what epithet the authority already quoted would apply to Jack in such a case. They look upon the farm as an unfailing source of revenue—as, come what may, a sure money-making institution—and that with the smallest possible personal industry or supervision. And yet most of such people are ambitious in a certain way. Grand displays at home and from home, aping the ways and habits of big people they have met or even seen, thoughtless expenditure in luxuries in diet and in dress,—all these are weaknesses frequently associated with the class of people here alluded to. No other person, of course, has any business with this matter, though any one is free to comment upon it; and when, along with the features indicated, there is an affectation of superiority—more commonly met with, it is right to add, in the wives and families of such farmers than in the farmers themselves—such people must not murmur if their peculiarities receive a passing notice. We know, however, Highland farmers, good men and true, who, in addition to diligently attending to their farms, are mindful of the cultivation of their minds and hearts, and their homes afford clear enough evidence of the cultured as well as practical views the heads of the house take of life and its duties.

Malcolm Macgregor, the tenant of Burnside farm, as was indicated, leads a busy life. Most farmers have what is called a manager—an official, as the name implies, supposed to supervise the farm interests generally. Some farmers specially need the services of such a person, their own practical knowledge being limited, or their fondness for work not being great; while others, having more than one farm, or one very large farm, require a manager, though they themselves may possess practical knowledge, and be fond of making themselves useful in their own interest. Malcolm Macgregor is his own manager, being fond of work and possessing the requisite practical knowledge, while the extent of his farm enables him to undertake its management. This renders Macgregor's life a particularly busy one. He goes "to the hill," confers with each shepherd, gives instructions, and, generally, conducts the intelligence department of the farm. In this respect it is a decided advantage to Magregor, who is a genuine Celt, that he can speak Gaelic, inasmuch as, though shepherds and other farm-servants unable to speak Gaelic are becoming numerous in Highland parishes, there are yet some that can better understand instructions conveyed in the Gaelic tongue.

Notwithstanding his busy professional life, Mr Macgregor finds time to give his services in the management of parochial work. He is a member of the School Board of Stratheden, and being of practical, shrewd business ways, is a useful member of the Board. In many Highland parishes those qualified for such offices are not particularly numerous, and the "munnistarrs" and the "big fairmers" in most of such cases have the work to do. Some of the latter are pleased with this arrangement—proud of it, indeed; and certain of the clergy even manifest a sort of eagerness for the dignity of office in school and other boards.

The average "big fairmer" in a Highland parish of to-day is not particularly given to going from home, or even to "calling" in his own neighbourhood. He travels to markets far and near, of course, goes to look for wintering for his sheep, and several times to see his sheep at wintering; but he does not often travel for travelling's sake. His calls in the parish are principally to other big farmers, and the usual conversation at such meetings is of sheep and wool, and the like, with an occasional reference to politics so called, to the laird, the rent, the parson, the preaching, the crofter, and the weather. It is said some big farmers like very much to speak about the parson in a way savouring of something like envy at "the cloth" for their position, and that such ones are particularly fond of trying to say smart, and even unkind, things about the clergy. Who knows but there may be some such persons?

—"big fairmers" are not known to be infallible more than any other people.

Malcolm Macgregor, however, appears to be very respectful to the clergy, attends church with praiseworthy regularity, and, so far as we have seen, manifests no tendency either to sneer at or envy the members of the clerical profession. The Rev. George Cameron, parish minister of Stratheden, is Mr Macgregor's pastor. It appears that the reverend gentleman and he were acquainted with each other long before either came to Stratheden, and when his reverence visits at Burnside, they like to repeat reminiscences of other days. They also talk of Church and other politics, and though of one mind on the Church question, it is said that, in the matter of politics so called, they do not always understand each other. The parson, so it is said, is what is called a Liberal-Conservative, and Macgregor is known as a pretty pronounced Liberal, which perhaps explains any political misunderstandings that may occur. But these two do not often talk of politics, nor, indeed, do politics so called by any means frequently form the subject of conversation between pastor and people in the average Highland parish.

With all his busy habits, and notwithstanding

that his industrious management of his farm necessitates his being much out of doors, Malcolm Macgregor is a thoroughly domesticated man, and a kind, and withal judicious, *paterfamilias*. We said that in the management of his surroundings Macgregor pays due regard to the æsthetic. This feature is specially noticeable within his home. There a not inconsiderable degree of refinement prevails. Not to speak of the minor element of elegance in furniture, we find Macgregor wisely encouraging the cultivation of the refining art of music; and more than once have we listened with pleasure to Malcolm and his little daughter Mary,—a bright, clever little lady, some eight years old, and doubly dear to Malcolm in his widowed loneliness—singing a plaintive little song or cheering hymn.

This reference to music leads us to mention that one of the members of Mr Malcolm Macgregor's household is Miss Flora Macleod, governess, an intelligent young lady, and a good musician. Governesses are not so numerous in Highland parishes as of old. Local schools are at hand, and where these are not considered sufficient, the increased travelling facilities afford easy access to boarding-schools and like institutions—both which facts may well enough be understood to tend towards diminishing the number of governesses. They yet are met with, however; and in many Highland parishes where what is called "the society" is somewhat limited, a governess is often a valuable accession to a family, and, indeed, to the neighbourhood generally. We spent an evening lately at Burnside Cottage, and heard Miss Macleod at the piano with much pleasure, while she gave, in fine style, some good old Scottish airs, some plaintive Highland melodies, and stirring pibrochs. Some young ladies, some Highland farmers' daughters among them—no one seems to know why—affect indifference to Scotch music generally, and Highland music in particular. We cannot help thinking that there must be something radically wrong in the training that would render such a feeble affectation as this possible; and we would respectfully warn patriotic parents and guardians in Highland parishes, to beware lest their daughters and their charge are kept in ignorance of the bettering strains of "the auld Scotch sangs" and plaintive Highland melodies by means of a false estimate of genuine culture.

Such is a "big fairmer," and such a "big fairmer's" home, in a Highland parish of to-day. There is no doubt that for a considerable period, up till some eight years ago, Highland farmers, in common with their brethren all over the country, enjoyed a large measure of prosperity. The general trade of the country—by which, obviously, the prices of cattle, sheep, and farm-produce generally are so much regulated—was brisk, foreign competition had not assumed the stupendous proportions it now presents, and the growing facilities for exporting local produce formed another element in giving to the Highland farmer a succession of, what even he himself admitted to be, very good years. The aspect of the farming situation is not, however, at this moment specially encouraging; and while some of the causes of this, such as the recent unusually severe winters—which have occasioned so much outlay for artificial feeding, and, it is to be feared, caused a deterioration in the sheep stock—may be expected to be temporary, signs are not wanting that, in the event of trade not markedly improving, and foreign competition even remaining at its present stage of development, the terms of farm occupancy will have to be practically considered by landlord and tenant. It must, of course, be borne in mind, that so long as farms to let are so eagerly sought after, as even yet they seem to be, by persons ready to give the same, if not a higher rent, landlords cannot reasonably be expected to offer such farms at a reduced rent. The matter, in short, will be self-adjusting. It is very much in the farmers' own hands, and will be regulated by the simplest rules of supply and demand.

No description of a farmer's surroundings would be complete without some reference to the farm-servants, on whom the general prosperity of a farm so much depends. The changed circumstances of shepherds and ploughmen consist mainly in their being, as compared with those of, say, thirty years ago, better educated and better paid. We have heard, however, a very shrewd "big fairmer" question the exclusive benefit of the change to servant or master, on the ground that—instances of which, he said, he had met with—the advance in education so called originates a sort of restless discontentedness and an impracticable ambition, and that the increased wages promote tastes and habits neither helpful to the usefulness of the servant nor favourable to the comfort of his home. Such results, no doubt, may occur; but it can hardly be doubted that the changes referred to, and especially the progress in education, must in the main tend towards the elevating and general improvement of the various classes of farm-servants.

Shepherds, as a class, seem better educated than ploughmen; and in the matter of speech and behaviour, a comparison would be decidedly in favour of the former. In the gathering of general information the shepherd seems more favourably circumstanced as to opportunity. His life, no doubt, is ordinarily as busy as the ploughman's, and at such seasons as lambing and clipping time, more exhausting, perhaps, than the ploughman makes his work at any time; while the latter knows nothing of an arduous, tedious, and even dangerous, employment the snows of winter sometimes throw in the shepherd's way. And yet the shepherd seems to find more opportunities for self-improvement than the ploughman, and that though the latter often is nearer any library that may chance to exist. While going his daily rounds from his mountain home, the shepherd, if so inclined, may take with him a book or newspaper, and sit, with his flock in view, on heathery knoll or rocky chair, and read amid the undisturbed and thought-begetting solitudes around him. And we have met shepherds in Stratheden, natives of the parish, men of some thirty years of age, who evidently do not neglect their opportunities of gathering information. We know two young shepherds on the farm of Heathfield, whom we consider to be good specimens of the better class of shepherds in a Highland parish of to-day. These are Kenneth Sutherland and Hugh Mackay, both sons of shepherds that long did duty on the same farm. These young men are sober, intelligent, and even thoughtful; nor would it be easy to find, among people of far greater pretensions, many so much at home on topics of general interest. Not, perhaps, that they are very strong in politics so called; but with the history of their country and the traditions of their parish, with the nature and prospects of the national industries, and such matters, they are acquainted to a degree that reflects much credit on their manner of using their opportunities. And in the matter of religious breadth, though it is difficult for them all at once to leap out of the narrow exclusiveness and self-righteous fanaticism encouraged by the local atmosphere in their early days, these young men manifest a hopeful progress. They adhere to the Free Church, for the reason, very probably, that, as a rule, determines the ecclesiastical name of people of any and every Church—because their parents attended the said Church; but their intelligence and growing knowledge of the world are manifested, not merely in their not being afraid to fraternise with " Moaderats," as some few of the older natives yet seem to be, but in the still greater advance indicated by their giving practical evidence that they do not fear—as some silly bigots seem to think—that their souls would be placed in jeopardy by their worshipping within the walls of a "Moaderat" kirk. We know another shepherd on the same farm of Heathfield—George Mackay to name, and some fifty years of age—who is as good a specimen of the intelligent shepherd as can easily be met with. He is fond of reading, and in his conversation generally manifests a shrewdness of observation, and an intelligent discernment, indicating good mental endowments, and a very diligent use of opportunities for exercising them.

In George Mackay there is traceable a peculiar combination of shyness and reflectiveness, which we have frequently noticed in shepherds—to be accounted for, perhaps, on the ground of the solitariness of their usual surroundings; and one can easily imagine how the isolation and silence of their mountain home, with the extent, and often the grandeur, of the prospect it commands, would combine to promote, if not shyness, at least a sort of quiet reserve, and something akin to contemplativeness. We recently heard from a clergyman in a Highland parish an amusing story, illustrative of the shyness in question. A shepherd about to get married, called on the reverend gentleman, soliciting his services in getting the nuptial knot tied. He sat for some time with the parson, but said nothing of his errand. He seemed to have something special to say, but, as our informant put it, "he never seemed able to come to the scratch." It was shyness, in short, and something more than the ordinary hesitancy some people display in such circumstances. At last he mustered courage so far, and thus abruptly addressed the reverend gentleman: "Please, sir, what's the size of your head, minister?" It is customary in some districts for the bridegroom to present the officiating clergyman with a hat, and hence the shy shepherd's rather remote way of announcing his errand!

We instanced the increase in wages as one of the changes in the circumstances of farm-servants generally, and by way of illustration of this marked change it may be mentioned, that while some forty years ago, and even at a later period, a ploughman's wages — exclusive of the usual perquisites of about seven bolls of oatmeal and a few bolls of potatoes yearly, as also a pint of milk daily — amounted to £7 in money yearly, the same class of ploughmen to-day, with the same perquisites, receive, as a rule, £20 per annum in money wages.

The style of living—in dress, diet, and general habits—is also considerably changed, and that very much in consequence of the increase in wages. Corduroy or moleskin, and the plainest homespun, were reckoned a suitable Sunday garb at the beginning of the period indicated. To-day these stuffs are, by the same class, considered too *common* for everyday wear even, and the finer tweeds alone meet the ambitious dress-taste of the average ploughman. Watches, now so common, were then exceedingly rare among this class,—so much so, that instances were known in which, among half-a-dozen ploughmen employed on the same farm, only one possessed the luxury of a watch to tell himself and his fellow-servants of the passing hours. To-day, it may be said, every ploughman has his watch; and herd-boys, not long able to know the language of a watch, consider themselves as not rightly equipped unless they sport their watch and albert chain,—and it is even said that in some such cases nought but the chain exists!

The change in the matter of diet is not so marked, if we except the increase in the use of tea and coffee; and altogether, it cannot be said that the increase in wages has brought about extravagance in diet. Butcher-meat, indeed, is nowadays much more sparingly used by farm-servants, and crofters also, than was common some fifty years ago, when the extensive outrun afforded more pasture than is to-day available; and to this, perhaps, combined with the now extensive use of tea and other commodities equally feeble in nutritive power, is owing the fact that the *physique* of the Highlander is not to-day, generally speaking, so hardy as of old. In certain aspects, however, there is a greater fastidiousness, so to speak, in the matter of diet. We heard an old ploughman say recently that he quite well remembers the time—some thirty-five years ago—when fish-sauce,—not the condiment popularly known as such, but the water in which fish is boiled,—was thought a palatable accompaniment to potatoes. To-day such, if offered, would be scornfully refused. Meal, milk, potatoes, fish, butter, and tea, constitute the staple articles of diet to-day. Tea is very generally used; and when farm-servants' wives—as like other wives they will do—meet for gossip, they must have tea with their tattle,—nor, at times, is the accompaniment of a liquid more intensely stimulating reckoned out of place at these conventicles.

Notwithstanding the greater outlay there may be

in diet, further explanation is necessary to show why, though farm-servants to-day receive so much higher wages, they are not, as a rule, more independent pecuniarily than in the days of lower wages. The explanation, it will be found, indicates a leaning in the direction of luxuries of various kinds. Ploughmen and their wives and children are to-day dressed in a fashion which necessitates a considerable inroad on the increase in the pay. Ploughmen are as proud as other people of seeing their wives well dressed, and both parents see no reason why their bairns should not be as elaborately costumed as other people's bairns. Besides, there are books—picture and other books—toys, and other modern articles, to be bought, which were comparatively unknown in other days, and this means another demand on the increase in the wages. To-day everything in dress must be *new*. In days gone by, when the ploughman's bairns needed clothes, old garments of older people were often turned to good account. Not so now to any great extent. The draper's shop is so accessible, and stuffs are so cheap, that there is a long account with the draper,—and hence yet another demand on the resources of the higher wages. Again, the ploughman's wife or grown-up daughter or son wishes to go from home a little distance, and who would be bothered walking even a couple of miles when the railway train is so convenient? Before the days of the railway a walk of eight or ten miles was little thought of by these people; but to-day two miles are considered a long way to walk; and hence—and people travel much more frequently to-day—one more outlet for the increased wages. These and similar considerations will explain why ploughmen that of old had but £7 per annum, with the usual perquisites, were, as a class, almost, if not altogether, as *rich* as those having to-day, with the same perquisites, £20 per annum of money wages. Some of them do save a little money, and in this way the ambition of some to become crofters is realised—the savings being expended in the purchase of stock and other requirements of the croft; but few farm-servants can manage to save enough to support them when no longer able to work. Farm-servants, however, and ploughmen especially, as a rule, do not long survive their working days; and in those cases in which incapacity for work overtakes an empty purse—if there be no grown-up sons able to help —parochial relief must be resorted to.

Of the general character of farm-servants it is not necessary to say much. As a class, they are sober and commendably industrious; of their moral character, strictly so called, the same complimentary verdict can hardly be so exclusively given. Without specifying certain aspects of an attractive moral life in which several of them are unhappily deficient, there is noticeable an unpleasant tendency to an objectionable, if not decidedly impure, style of speech; and too often the kind of wit considered smartest by people of this class is vulgar, and occasionally strong in impure suggestiveness. This is more generally the case in regard to ploughmen —shepherds being, as a rule, superior to ploughmen, not only in general intelligence, but likewise in manner, speech, and general behaviour. Masters are more responsible for the moral training of those ploughmen and other farm-servants than certain of these masters seem to realise; and we have sometimes thought these latter, like some other people, might profitably consider what name is given, in a Book that masters and servants profess to reverence, to not doing good when one "knoweth to do" it. There are, of course, among farm-servants, persons of excellent moral character, who are also intelligent and well-informed; but there are likewise among them individuals sadly low in the scale of morality and intelligence,—

and the problem of raising such in the former scale is one that perplexes many genuinely interested in their welfare. A large-hearted, manly interest taken by masters in servants would go far to encourage the latter in well-doing; and where such interest exists, its good effect is reflected in the general character of the servants. Some masters in Highland parishes, as in other places, seem to take little or no interest in those in their employment, and even speak of them as if they were of a lower order of being. The existence between them of such a gulf as this indicates is not hopeful, and with regard to such masters, it is difficult to check a feeling of contemptuous scorn when one hears them speaking slightingly of their servants, while doing nothing to promote their moral and social welfare. The dignity that comes of genuine culture is never compromised in the endeavour to improve a fellow-creature; but while it is gratifying to know that there are not a few masters who manifest an intelligent appreciation of their duty to their servants, there are cases in which a feeble affectation of superiority renders a master indifferent, if not blind, to this important duty.

CHAPTER X.

THE USUAL VISITORS TO A HIGHLAND PARISH.

To look at Stratheden, its normal aspect seems one of undisturbed seclusion, so far as visitors are concerned. And yet it is visited, and that largely compared with thirty years ago,—this change, like many others referred to, having been brought about very much by the growing facilities of communication. Besides sportsmen and "great guns" in other fields, there come regularly commercial travellers—an apparently industrious class of persons—and there likewise visit us tourists, tramps, and tinkers — the visits from the two latter fraternities being more frequent than the average resident cares about. Though by no means least, we elect to speak of sportsmen last, for a reason which, while valid in our own eyes, may seem slender enough to *priority* hunters among sportsmen; for doubtless even among them men wishing to be first will be found. The Twelfth of August is the orthodox date of the sportsman's first outing. Tramps and tinkers arrive long before then; and indeed we ourselves have been honoured with a visit from representatives of the two latter communities as early as the first, not of August merely, but even of January. Tourists, specially so called, and commercial travellers likewise, are earlier arrivals than the worshippers of Saint Grouse and kindred idols. So then, in the matter of order of treatment, we avoid the delicate question of precedence, and for the nonce adopt the rule of "first come, first described."

Tramps of various sorts come to Stratheden at all seasons and in all weathers, and—especially in summer and autumn—in perplexingly large numbers. The mainland districts, of course, are more largely visited by them, certain of the outer islands enjoying a privileged immunity from this species of infliction. The tramp is an almost daily visitor, and often he who calls early in the day is but the pioneer of more to follow, many tramps arranging to come to districts in bands. We happened in a very harmless way recently to observe to a tramp, in a sort of inquiring manner, that we thought the class of people he belonged to travelled in *bands*. He denied the fact in the bold style that the average tramp adopts when displeased; and, bolder still, he proceeded to remark that he himself had never been in Stratheden before,—the fact being that he had visited the parish twice within the preceding six months. The recent commercial depression caused a great increase in the tramp department, or at least it supplied many with an introductory ground of appeal. "Out of work," "trade dull," "got my hand crushed," "got my leg broken," "fell ill," are some of the stock introductory phrases popular among them; but few, if any, that study their ways believe their statements—an incredulity warranted by the tramp's very frequent disregard of truth. To judge from the number coming, and the frequency of their visits, one would suppose tramps do a flourishing business in Stratheden; and indeed we are glad to be able to chronicle that Highlanders generally lean in the direction of taking a practical compassion on the wandering homeless poor. Some tramps obviously enough need help, whether they deserve it or not,—old broken-down men, and young but old-looking men, with a shattered miserable look painfully suggestive of the hard ways of the transgressor. Some are essentially bad-looking fellows, with a cast of face indicating some capacity for roughness and cunning;

and though, as a rule, they make no distinctly violent displays, a refusal of help at times discovers some leanings that way. Such as are believed to be deserving are usually helped. There are some of them one can easily pronounce undeserving—the saucy, growling grumblers that refuse to take meat instead of money. Individuals of this ungrateful type refuse such food as bread and milk, fish, and meal, apparently thinking no other help than hard cash worth having. The Stratheden crofters and others in the parish rarely would send a tramp away unhelped; but the tramp's preference for the compact coin cannot always be satisfied by the average resident. A refusal of help—of money help, that is—occasionally gives rise to a ludicrous though unpleasant scene. The unsatisfied tramp gets angry, and gives vent to his feelings in the offensive slang in which most of the fraternity seem well versed. The refusing party, as happens now and then, is more at home in Gaelic than English, and responds with more or less bitterness in the former language, of which the tramp is ignorant. Of one mind for the moment—that is, in being angry with each other—they employ different languages, but seem, however, to succeed in rousing each other's anger as well as relieving their own feelings.

Tramps have various ways of finding lodgings for the night. In summer and autumn, ordinarily, this matter is not reckoned problematic by themselves. Most of them then select a grassy bed in some sheltered spot, and with nought between them and the sky, in this wide berth await the morn. Some will select a cart-shed for a sleeping apartment; and a Stratheden crofter told us of his having one morning last autumn found a tramp asleep in his cart, and that with a soundness that some accustomed to better or softer beds might envy. Many of these tramps are very much afraid of horses and cattle, and in selecting the sort of wide berth referred to, they are careful to see that these quadrupeds have a field for themselves, —careful to give them, in other words, a very "wide berth." A tramp came to us in great distress one evening lately, begging for old clothes. He related a mishap that befell him, and on which he grounded an urgent appeal for clothes. He was, to give his own story, passing through a park belonging to a Stratheden farmer, and a certain quadruped (a perfectly harmless heifer, we were afterwards told) seemed anxious to interview the tramp, and even make, as the alarmed vagrant believed, a decidedly definite appeal to his feelings. The tramp did not reciprocate the heifer's attentions, and proceeded to retire from the field. Gathering speed, though losing coolness, as he fled from the quadruped, he reached a wire fence, once over which he would be safe. In leaping the fence, the poor tramp, unnecessarily frightened—for he never looked back to see that the heifer gave up the chase, if it ever really began it—got entangled somehow in the fence, and a piece of broken wire did serious damage to his clothes. Hence his urgent appeal to us for clothes. When the weather prevents the tramp occupying the large sort of bed alluded to, other lodgings must be got. In Stratheden there are a few houses that afford shelter for a few pence—threepence usually—per night; and those that either will not or cannot give even this small sum try to find a bed in some open outhouse or other available corner.

Adhering to the precedence of early arrival in our description of visitors, after tramps, specially so called, come tinkers, well known in all Highland parishes. Some of these latter come as early as the tramps; but the important fact is that both come earlier than is ordinarily relished, and certainly oftener than is liked. In Stratheden there are at times no fewer than half-a-dozen tinker camps. It is common enough, on a calm morning, to see smoke rising from three or four tents pitched in sheltered nooks along the Strath. These tinkers seem to like the sheltered woods of Stratheden. In the best-kept woods even, there will always be some firewood available, which is an important consideration from the tinker point of view; and the running stream in the wood is another advantage when clothes are to be washed, and when the rarer exercise of personal ablution is indulged in.

The prevailing tinker names are Stewart, Macphee, Macneil, and Macalister. The Stewarts consider themselves the representatives of the older and better type of the tinker tribe, and this contention now and then develops into contentions of a more violent sort. These latter contentions, as a rule, are settled, or rather, for the time, finished, in the pronounced and rather disgusting fashion deemed orthodox by the fraternity. Not that *big* fights are common among the tinkers frequenting Stratheden. Of course they have their domestic squabbles, as some other people not ordinarily called tinkers have; but it is doubtful if these are as bitter, and especially as permanent in their results, as the squabbles of those that consider themselves better than tinkers.

The Macneils, despite the pride of name displayed by the Stewarts, look down on the latter. The former, undoubtedly, not only have a more civilised look about them, but exhibit something like leanings towards settled or "housed" ways of livings. The Macneils and Macalisters do no small traffic in horse-dealing; and some of the Stratheden people, though dubious as to the safety of trafficking with tinkers, accept the risk and buy, or, as is often the case, exchange horses with them.

The children of the camp, always remarkably numerous, seem almost uncared for, though in not a few cases this is more apparent than real. Although, as among other people, some scenes of more or less frequent occurrence seem to indicate a scantiness of affection for relatives among tinkers, they have their feelings, of course, as the saying is; and instances of this are met with. Some time ago the son of a tinker, at the time camped in Stratheden, died, and the sad, heart-broken look of his father's face for long after amply proved that, however much despised by many, they are not insensible to the influence of natural affection. Last spring, while taking a walk one evening along a road in Stratheden, we heard in the distance the bagpipes sounding, and, liking the stirring strains, we naturally wished to know whence they issued. Our curiosity was soon set at rest. A little farther on from where we first heard the music there is a quarry, in which at the time there was a tinker camp—and there, a few yards from the camp, to bagpipe-music played by their father, danced two tinker children, brother and sister, player and dancers looking as happy as could be. The scene was suggestive in many ways, but we must not wait to moralise. Often in the coldest weather tinkers' children run about barefooted, but never seem to feel cold. Poor children! they thrive wonderfully, and it is almost miraculous that they do so, considering the hardships they have to endure in their too early wanderings. By a strange reversing of the ordinary arrangement, the children of a tinker camp are often the principal providers of the food of the family. The people of Stratheden are well aware how largely the commissariat department of the camp is intrusted to the tinker begging-children. The older members of the family are not above begging; but while the tinkers' bairns are commissioned to beg meal, butter, tea, sugar, and milk, the former devote special attention to providing, by begging from "big fairmer" or small crofter, hay, straw, and oats for their horses.

Tinkers have been known to attend church in Stratheden, but they are not strong in church-going; and we have often wondered whether their sense of the estimate, ordinarily very low, formed of them by outsiders, has anything to do with their very rare frequenting of church. But this suggests a large subject, and we proceed to observe, that though not given to church-going, they affect ecclesiastical designations, and very irreverently, as do some others not ordinarily called tinkers, introduce these designations into their fights and squabbles generally. Some of them say they are Protestants, while others allege they are Roman Catholics; and in a rather big fight that took place a few months ago in a parish near Stratheden, where tinker representatives of each faith were engaged, they were calling each other by the various ecclesiastical names, with prefixes, and affixes too, of very violent and disgusting import. The same *feeling* perhaps may be easily enough met with in more refined communities—but then tinkers have their own way of squabbling; and though refined people, so called, might desire to give like definite and *striking* expression to the feeling—the ecclesiastical feeling, we mean—it is well it is not fashionable.

Their wandering life, while unfavourable to church-going, is particularly injurious in regard to the education of their children. In fact their children are hardly ever educated—and the best way of getting them educated constitutes a somewhat difficult problem. But though perplexing as it stands, the problem is not unhopefully so, when it is considered that the tinker system shows signs of yielding to the changes of to-day. Some tinkers' sons, encouraged by the travelling facilities of these days, and not quite ignorant of ambition, are taking to more civilised, settled ways of living; and this itself, among a people at one time so very exclusive and isolated, is significant as to the future. Then, again, the tin dishes and other articles sold by tinkers can now be so easily had elsewhere, that the tin specialty which long sustained many a camp will gradually cease to have its effect. And there is a reason of quite a different kind for thinking the system is destined to break up. Notwithstanding that occasionally a stalwart frame is seen among them, on many may be seen an ominous enough look of physical feebleness. Frequent exposure to wet and cold, scanty clothing and little food, in addition to intemperate habits, have made deterioration evident enough in not a few cases—a fact which encourages the belief that the distinctiveness of the fraternity will gradually be modified, and probably, in the not very distant future, altogether cease to hold. To render this more probable, it need only be added that within recent years some tinkers, previously known in Stratheden in their wandering ways, have taken to a stationary mode of life, and now occupy settled homes.

Adhering to our rule as to priority of treatment, commercial travellers would now be referred to. They, however, have been spoken of in the chapter on "Shopkeeping," and other than what is there indicated, there is no feature of special interest in the commercial traveller's relation to the average Highland parish.

Next in order of treatment come tourists. They are far behind tramps and tinkers—as to date of arrival, that is to say. Tourists pass and repass in increasing numbers from the beginning of July until the end of September. Many of them wait to luxuriate amid the stillness and the grand scenery of Stratheden. Though there is not much, if any, of what is popularly known as the "lion" element to be seen in Stratheden, there are shaggy mountain-brows and bold faces of gigantic rocks; and though no grand triumphs of architectural skill are visible, who knows but the chronicler of the future may have something great to say of Stratheden in this respect—a future, too, not far distant? There is as wide a gulf between some of the cottages of to-day and the huts of fifty years ago, as there is between the former and certain structures daily visited as triumphs of architecture. But there are at this moment in Stratheden curiosities of architecture, models, in their way, of design and build. There are one or two specimens of huts, of a kind common fifty years ago, yet lingering, and perhaps the like of them may never have been seen by some that travel far in quest of "lions." Not that they are squalid: the average Highland parish stands tolerably high in the matter of cleanliness, whatever may be said of the godliness to which it is said cleanliness is so nearly allied. Nor are these huts devoid of comfort of a kind; and indeed, so far as dryness and warmth are concerned, they are superior to some more elaborate structures. The fabrics we allude to are peculiar for their sunk-flat appearance, their scanty light and defective ventilation, and the very rare contrivances for securing both. This sort of building, already sunken in its look, will soon utterly sink out of view; but by those among visitors to Highland parishes who wish to study the history of an interesting people and country, such buildings will be thought at least worth looking at. To certain tourists they ought to possess a fond interest. Many that first saw the light in such a home are to-day occupying influential and lucrative situations in various parts of the country. Some of these make a point of occasionally visiting the scene of early days; and all such, except those afflicted with a contemptible emptiness of head and heart, will give a fond lingering look at "the auld hoose," if it yet endures; and should *their* dear auld hoose have yielded to the removing influence of time, there is a sort of satisfying of the commendable feeling alluded to in even looking at any similar humble habitation yet "to the fore."

As was to be expected, the new means of locomotion have increased the number of tourists, and there has been much commendable enterprise displayed to meet the increasing strain on the means of communication between southern districts and the Northern Highlands generally. The Highland Railway Company, and the owners of the excellent and admirably managed fleet of steam-ships known in the West Highlands as "the Hutchesons'" steamers — the Messrs Hutcheson have a very worthy successor in Mr Macbrayne — have so efficiently contributed their respective shares to the establishing of rapid and easy communication, that to-day the proverbial distance "from Land's End to John o' Groat's" may be travelled in little over twenty-four hours; and Oban, Skye, Strathpeffer, and other places deservedly famous for health-giving qualities and richly varied scenery, are brought within easy access. Oban, so much nearer the south now that the Oban and Callander Railway is open, forms an excellent centre for pleasant and interesting excursions by sea and land, and is also valued by many as a bathing-place; while for such as are neither on excursions nor on bathing bent, Oban is an attractive place to linger in for a week or two. Skye, so long and so deservedly enjoying an established reputation among tourists in quest of scenery and health, continues to grow in favour, because the travelling facilities are bringing it within more convenient reach and making it better known; and enterprising endeavours are being made to meet the growing demand for hotel accommodation in this beautiful "isle of the west."

There is, of course, very considerable variety in the tourist element. It is not, however, necessary to detail this variety, as it is not a feature peculiar to tourists visiting Highland parishes. Suffice it to say, there come big and little men, literally and figuratively; and it is amusing enough to notice those tourists whose conscious looks and general air suggest that they feel very big on the strength of the mere fact of being tourists. There was a time when more than now this vain conceit was satisfied. This was when tourists were rare, and the average Highlander's views of the world generally somewhat narrow and hazy—flash, glitter, and tall talk having then a tendency to command the wonderment of the poorer Highlanders in their humble obscurity. And yet the conscious ones continue to come, and probably will do so, although the *vision* and discriminating powers of the average Highlander are becoming daily enlarged. But, of course, tourists with the conscious leaning are but a proportion — a small proportion, let it be gratefully noted—of the many annually flocking to the Highlands. Family groups, solitary bachelors and groups of bachelors, elderly maiden ladies singly and in groups, generally speaking, make up the usual tourists; and there are city merchants, lawyers, clergymen, medical men, landed proprietors, and persons of no occupation, among the number. The city pastor, exhausted with sermon-making, and especially with visiting his flock and attending to the other usual and ordinary duties, comes to get up renewed vigour of mind and body. Sometimes a conscious parson may be seen strutting along in a very large way; but it is only just to "the cloth" to say such parsons are rare—which is a special cause of thankfulness. Tradesmen, clerks, salesmen, and suchlike, form no small proportion of the tourist family. So far as some of this latter section are concerned, one likes to think that the praiseworthy ambition of visiting places of interest, historical and otherwise, encourages the prudent economy necessary to enable them to do some "touristing"—more especially as many of them have a tired look, which, however, fresh air and distance from the desk and the often dingy office, soon scare. Others look not tired, but tiresome—very, very big individuals, elaborately done up, and affecting the later development of the "swell" idea.

Special reference must be made to a remarkable specimen of the tourist fraternity quite within the range of our subject,—we mean the native Highlander who has been some years away, and who, coming in tourist fashion to revisit the old place, affects ignorance of all matters Highland — language, customs, opinions, and suchlike — evidently with the view to his being thought superior to what he, in his empty way, calls these far-back, poor, superstitious Highlanders. This sort of personage will be thought more contemptible when it is borne in mind that his wish is to conceal the fact that he spent no small portion of his early life in one of those "dreadfully black and little huts" he talks about so disparagingly and feebly. But there are other "Highland laddies" of a wiser, manlier sort. These, in early life, go to push their fortune in one or other of the southern towns, and succeed, — Highlanders have a way of succeeding,—and it is a settled resolve with them that their native parish be revisited periodically; and if those that made the "old home" dear are gone, there is a saddened satisfaction in revisiting the very heather, and the rocks, and the bonnie burn "clear winding still," near which stood the home of early days. Those we speak of have not forgot their Gaelic, as some ones of the weaker sort affect to do; and, impressed with memories of days of yore, they like to speak it with such as may happen to know it—while the latter speak to them of the old people and ways, alluding, half sorrowfully it may be, to the changed aspect of to-day.

In addition to the benefits gained by tourists themselves in their Highland rambles, certain of the natives and others are benefited by the tourist system in respect of the circulation of money thus caused. Where no "boots" forms one of the appliances and means of the Highland inn, and where, should such exist, the pressure of the busy season renders "boots" unable to *run* to the occasion, some boys and grown-up lads in Highland parishes make rather a good thing of it during the season by carrying luggage and going messages for tourists. Then some tourists go a-fishing, and this means employment for such as we refer to. And again, some tourist of antiquarian or geologic leaning goes for a ramble among the rocks in the hope of a precious "find," and he must needs take one of the village boys to carry the collection; and hence to such boy a find much more fondly prized by him than the treasure intrusted to him by his temporary employer. Some of our readers may have read or heard of an incident recorded as having taken place in the Highlands, and which shows how a tourist of this latter description was pretty decidedly done by a man whom he employed in the capacity indicated. To the best of our recollection the main circumstances are these: The tourist, an enthusiastic student of lithology, left a Highland inn one summer morning to search for precious stones near a rocky hill some fourteen miles away. He was accompanied by a native Highlander—a calculating, cute sort of man; but so far as the metals prized by his employer were concerned, *stone-blind*. In the course of the day various stones of the precious sort were gathered, which were deposited in a strong canvas or leather bag carried by the hired man. In the evening the two parted, the tourist giving specific instructions to his attendant to take the stones to the inn. Feeling the precious metals rather a burden, the Highlander adopted the very simple expedient of throwing all the stones away, thinking it foolish indeed to carry a burden of stones fourteen miles, when there were so many stones quite as good just beside the inn! Arrived at the inn with the empty bag, he filled it to the original apparent bulk with *very, very* common stones, not certainly classified among precious stones, which treasure he ordered to be given to the enthusiastic student of lithology on his return!

In pursuance of our order of treatment as determined by date of arrival, we now proceed to say a few words of sportsmen. To some sportsmen the very difficulty of travelling to and in the Highlands long ago used to be an additional attraction in respect of that difficulty satisfying adventurous leanings; but notwithstanding this, the number of sportsmen coming to the Highlands is larger since the travelling facilities have been increased. There are several shooting-boxes in Stratheden—the district being not a little famous for its attractiveness in this respect. Since the railway was extended to the district, one or two pretty-looking shooting-lodges have gone up in the parish; and early in August the ordinarily quiet railway station of Stratheden for a few days presents a thronged and bustling aspect. As in other places, there is no small variety of rank and intellect discernible in this annual accession to the population. Including the lessees of the shootings and their guests, there are earls and lords not a few, esquires too numerous to mention, and parsons — chiefly from south of the Tweed—in wellnigh amazing abundance.

Many of the natives view with special horror the fact of "munnistarrs going to the hull to be shooting and running aifter the birds." Some such natives, aiming at being sarcastic, may now and then be heard saying — "Graysheous me! what would the godly people *before* say if they would be seeing munnistarrs running like mat people with fire and powter? I wonder whatna place in the Bible tells them to be shooting and work like that? They're saying they will be going on their knees in the hull for birds and the like o' that. Am afraid it's no on their knees where they should be they'll be." Nor is it the uneducated alone that make comments of this sort. A Free Church clergyman not sixty miles from Stratheden, and seemingly not disposed to think kindly of the sportsman institution generally, a short time ago, in referring to sportsmen, ended some strong remarks with the following silly, but, as he believed, triumphant sarcasm: "I wonder how many gamekeepers Moses had?" We trust it is not beyond our province to express the hope that this game problem, started by the divine referred to, will not be thought of sufficient importance to engage the attention of the competent Church judicatories, already amply agitated anent themes where Moses is concerned.

Besides the class of persons indicated, tea-planters from India and China, prosperous city merchants from Glasgow, Edinburgh, and London, bankers of various stamps, retired grocers from all quarters, and not a few cultured disciples of the pen and the pencil, may be found among the many sportsmen annually visiting the Highlands. It is unnecessary to say much anent the variety of intellect observable. As among other people, there are among them men of mind, and men very scantily endowed with brains; persons of mediocrity, and some a degree higher than the ordinary level; and as is true of tourists, there are "conscious" ones among sportsmen also, these latter being very big persons. Ordinarily, however, the repose of culture is to be seen among sportsmen, though stupidity, and even vulgarity, have each representatives among them.

In inquiring what influence the annual accession of sportsmen has on the average Highland parish, there is no doubt that the most prominent, and certainly the most definite result, is the circulation of money thus caused; and so far, at least, they do good to others. The average native resident had long been in the habit of reckoning sportsmen veritable "mints,"—visitors with unlimited ability, and a constant readiness, to give away money. This delusion may now be almost pronounced extinct; and it is much the same with the feeling of something like awe with which sportsmen used to be viewed by the average native of long ago, as being in every case not only extraordinarily rich, but great and powerful, and everything that was impressive. Of course, the rich, and the great too, are to-day among sportsmen as of old, and so also are the good and the true; but the penny paper and cheap literature generally, and the widening view encouraged by this and the travelling facilities of to-day, are combining to invest the local estimate of sportsmen with a more sensible, discerning, and, consequently, a more independent character. Nor, so far as some sportsmen are concerned, would their estimate of the natives be the worse of modification. Some of the less thoughtful and cultured of sportsmen are too prone to be influenced by the "inferior clay" idea, and to discard certain harmless local prejudices, in such matters, for instance, as Sunday observance. We know well enough, and, we think, have shown in another chapter, that the Highland estimate of what right Sunday observance is has often been—and is, to this day, in some cases—very unsound and even superstitious; but those among sportsmen and others who know that all healthy development requires time, and who understand that toleration is a mutual duty, will studiously avoid giving needless offence. Many sportsmen wisely do so, we gladly chronicle,—giving practical evidence of their belief that Christian charity forbids giving countenance to aught that unnecessarily hurts the harmless prejudices of even the sensitively weak. And besides this, of many sportsmen it must be recorded to their credit, that they give ample evidence, by kindly interest and deeds of active benevolence, that they are wishful to render their stay in the Highlands not merely a source of satisfaction to themselves, but likewise a source of profit and happiness to others.

Speaking of sportsmen, it is right that reference be made to gamekeepers and gillies. Shepherds and ploughmen are in the habit of saying that gamekeepers have grand times of it,—by which is meant that the latter have little to do, and that, by regular wages and the gratuities of the shooting season, their pecuniary advantages are great. No doubt, except for some weeks from and after "the Twelfth," the duties of the gamekeeper are not too arduous. He is very much his own master; nor is this privilege seriously interfered with, even where there is a head-gamekeeper understood to supervise two or three subordinates. He must, of course, take occasional runs over the "ground" to see what is doing; and he is in duty bound to beware lest aspiring ones, ambitious after even temporary game-keepership—on poaching bent, in other words—are on the scent for game,—which extent of work, however, does not mean much in the nature of arduous toil. But the gamekeeper's duties from and after "the Twelfth," until, say, early in October, are, as a rule, heavy enough. Early astir, a long journey, hard and constant work, and long hours, and this repeated day after day, is no joke. Generally speaking, however, the sportsman is very mindful of the gamekeeper's requirements in the busy season ; and in the matter of food and drink, liberal provision is made for gamekeepers and gillies. These officials, gamekeepers especially, acquire a sort of smartness of manner, and particularly, as they themselves think, of speech, by associating with sportsmen; and it is very amusing to hear some of them affect a sort of "tall," grand talk — the amusement being intensified by the occasional *natural* spicing of the Highland accent with which it is interspersed. Some gamekeepers are essentially pawky, and, though appearing very unassuming and receptive while in the hill with sportsmen, are known to be carefully studying the individual characters, as also, with apparent humility and guilelessness, humouring the peculiarities of the several sportsmen, and especially feeding the vanity of the vain among them. In the case of such sportsmen as are quick to hear of local matters, it is doubtful whether, in accepting the gamekeeper's version, the former always exercise a prudent discretion by making allowance for local prejudices and envyings. It is pretty well known that, in local ecclesiastical matters especially, some sportsmen are often materially deceived by the one-sided narrative of a bigoted gamekeeper. To know aright, sportsmen must either inquire of ones less likely to be narrowly prejudiced, or, better still, wait to be able to judge for themselves.

Besides gamekeepers and gillies, many natives get work during the shooting season—so that in this way, to others than themselves, the coming of sportsmen brings at least one tangible benefit; but as to the measure of affection those thus employed cherish for their employers, and as to the other and larger question of the sentiments with which the average native views sportsmen, we need not here inquire. We cannot help, however, expressing the hope that, whatever extension of the sportsman system may be contemplated, a wise, generous regard will be paid to the welfare of farmers and crofters—both which classes, we maintain, with every reasonable appreciation of the benefits conferred by sportsmen, contribute so much to the strength and prosperity of the country.

CHAPTER XI.

BIG DAYS IN A HIGHLAND PARISH.

THE "big" days in the average Highland parish are not numerous. Monotonous sameness has almost universal sway, and such days as show any features different from the ordinary round may be briefly told.

Fairs will naturally occur to many as likely to hold a high place among such "big" days as may exist. The fair—or the "markatt," as some of the older natives call it—was for a long time a great institution in the Highlands. In most Highland parishes, indeed, up till within the last fifteen years or so, it was the only big day, or series of days, for the "markatt" often extended over two, and even three, days. Of course, the Communion season was then, as it yet is, looked upon by very many as a great event,—not chiefly because of the grander thoughts it is calculated to suggest, but as a time for meeting relatives and acquaintance, for purposes of getting news and exchanging gossip, which latter was often unprofitable enough. No doubt there were many then—more, perhaps, than to-day—who looked forward to the Communion season under the inspiration of feelings appropriate to the event; but of the other sort there were, and are, many, as all that know the Highlands are aware.

The "markatt," however, was *the* big day properly so called. It suggested no idea of restraint, no necessity for assumed gravity of demeanour, and was therefore more generally and eagerly looked forward to as a big day. There were, of course, as is yet the case, only a few parishes that could claim the dignity of having a market "stance," and to which the people flocked from the surrounding districts. One locality was the market-place for some six or seven parishes, and, generally speaking, the "markatt" took place twice a-year. It usually began on a Tuesday, and often extended over three days. The first day was the principal business-day,— the day on which the buying and selling of cattle and horses took place. The Wednesday turn-out partook greatly of the character of variety. Lads and lasses were out in strong force, and, just as to-day, there was no small flirtation — in some cases very demonstrative. The Wednesday of the market was a general holiday, and shepherds, ploughmen, and others, with their wives and families, strolled along—the young people looking with special interest at the "sweetie"-vendor's spread, the temporary toy-shop, the merry-go-round, and a few other attractions. Towards evening some in the crowd displayed leanings in the direction of boisterousness, as the result of too frequent visits to the "tent" or extemporised dram-shop; and later on, some of the boisterous ones might be found figuring prominently at something of the nature of a free fight, at which wild and often disgusting exclamations largely prevailed.

The "markatt" of to-day, in many respects, is much the same as it was at the period referred to. There are changes, however. The market is not to-day so prolonged an event, so far especially as districts having railway communication are concerned; and this is well, because those that remained longest were ones, as a rule, under the spell of a decidedly injurious attraction—strong drink. Not that they were perhaps drunkards, but in meeting friends, or closing a bargain, they got into tasting, and unfortunately tasting too much. The railway in this respect has been, and is, a temperance reformer. The people may leave home in the morning for the market, buy and sell, see friends and acquaintance, visit the "sweetie" stall, hear the strolling violin-player, and return home by train the same day. Again, the attendance at the market of to-day is not quite so large as of old. The travelling facilities of the present time explain this. When travelling was difficult, and especially when trains and steamers were comparatively unknown, the people looked on the market as a time to meet to transact the greater part of the business of the year. Now it is different. The train is so convenient that people can go from home at any time. Then where no train is, the steamer, and where neither is accessible, the mail-coach, facilitates going from home at any time,—and altogether the "markatt" gathering has become a secondary event.

We remember one or two big days of some twenty years ago, and even later, that are now swamped in the changes of to-day. There was the examination of the parish school by the Church dignitaries of the district, and which took place once a-year. The examination, which was conducted by the parish minister and one or two of the neighbouring clergy, was long and eagerly, if not anxiously, looked forward to by the scholars. Parents came out in considerable force in those days to witness the event; and, as with the pupils themselves, on the examination-day some parents were proud and some disappointed, and, doubtless, a few envious. Under the new system the examination or inspection day is not, to outsiders at least, so great an event. To the teacher, no doubt, it is quite as important a day—perhaps, indeed, in some cases more so—as her Majesty's Inspector of Schools does not necessarily accept the indulgent estimate of the school's appearance which some of the clergy may have been wont to take. Be this as it may, in the average Highland parish the examination by the inspector does not seem to be attended by nearly so many parents and others as used to be present on the examination-day under the old system. We wish to take this opportunity of testifying to the very general satisfaction which the school inspectors visiting the Northern Highlands afford in these districts. They are all gentlemen of ability and culture, and undoubted integrity; and the fact of their being Highlanders, and so knowing the ways, and what yet is, to some extent, the language of the Highlander, constitutes an additional element of efficiency in this highly important department of our educational arrangements.

We remember another big day of some twenty years ago, not now so big, to all appearance—the great parish shinty-match which took place on Old Christmas Day or Old New-Year's Day. It may have been confined to certain districts; but, even where we knew it then as very popular and largely honoured, it seems to-day to have very much faded as an annual institution. Of course, shinty is popular among boys in every Highland parish; but the day alluded to was a big day to which old boys as well as young looked forward, and on which many spectators turned out to witness the trial of strategy and speed. Shinty competitions on a somewhat large scale yet take place in some Highland parishes; but whatever be the cause—whether it is that the accession of strangers has introduced newer fashions, or that volunteer shooting-competitions may in some cases have swamped the shinty-matches—these latter do not to-day seem to be so general or so popular as at the time specified.

The comparatively modern institution of volunteering gives rise to one or two big days in some parishes. A volunteer corps now flourishes in many Highland parishes, and, as a rule, a fine-looking set of volunteers these parishes command. We have a corps in Stratheden, over fourscore strong—generally speaking, a stalwart, handsome set of men; and who will blame the Stratheden people if they speak with pride of the creditable appearance the Stratheden Volunteer Corps usually makes at the annual inspection by the captain—a young nobleman in the neighbourhood, deservedly esteemed by the Stratheden volunteers—and at the big review that yearly takes place in the district? The Stratheden volunteers have big days—such as the captain's inspection, friendly matches between married and single men, Christmas competitions, and the like,—all, comparatively speaking, modern big days in the Highlands.

We had another big day, or rather big night, in Stratheden lately—very big, indeed, because the first of the kind in the parish. It was a concert got up by local talent, and the singers at which were almost all natives. Some enthusiastic Celts, naturally enough, missed the Gaelic element from the songs; and, though the singing of Gaelic songs is becoming very rare, it is said the programme of the next concert will contain one Gaelic song at least.

Another big day in Stratheden is the railway excursion day—"La'n Scurshan," as some of the older people call the cheap-fare day in the Gaelic tongue. This, of course, is comparatively modern, and is largely patronised, being a day to which many in the parish look forward long and eagerly. Some go as far as Glasgow or Edinburgh, but the great majority content themselves with visiting friends some ten miles, or thereabouts, distant.

Another big day seems to be—it is an ecclesiastical day—the day of signing the "call" to a clergyman selected to fill a vacant charge. It has already been noticed that the great majority of the native residents in Highland parishes adhere to the Free Church, and hence it is to this Church our remarks in this instance refer. We have seen on such a day the neighbourhood where the event of signing the call was taking place very largely peopled, giving the day a very big appearance indeed. Lessons of the fickleness of crowds, however, may be gathered from contrasting this apparent enthusiasm with events that take place afterwards in the relations between these eager-looking "calling" ones, and their, for the nonce at least, popular, very popular pastor. We remember, some half-dozen years ago, seeing a very large crowd assembled in a Highland parish for the purpose of signing the call to a clergyman who, when candidating, made a very great impression. A year passed, and another year went with it, but by this time more than time was vanishing. The preacher's popularity was fading; and whoever was to blame—we suspect the fickleness of the multitude had more to do with it than any collapse in the preacher's powers—by the time three years had passed we believe there would be a not inconsiderable number of the original and enthusiastic crowd quite prepared to turn out to *call* upon their pastor to vacate his charge. We need not wait to make reflections on the cooling of the enthusiasm of the big day of a call-signing. We cannot help remarking, however, that it would be unwise, in every case, to put it down to any want of sincerity at the time of signing, for Highlanders are just as sincere, as honest, as any other people. The fact, however, of their being easily led, and especially so in matters ecclesiastical, may partly explain such a phenomenon as we refer to.

Another big day is the crofters' rent-day — on which, usually, no small excitement is observable. As a rule, there is a praiseworthy ambition to be prepared for this day; and as the crofters pass homewards after paying their rents, there is, in many cases, discernible the commendable consciousness of duty done. In no district that we know of is the crofter's rent high, and it should be, generally speaking, an easy matter to meet the requirements of this big day.

Such are the principal "big" days in the average Highland parish of to-day.

In some central districts with special privileges, games, such as tossing the caber, dancing, and suchlike, take place at stated seasons; but those other events we have referred to include the big days generally known in the Highlands of to-day.

CHAPTER XII.

CONCLUSION.

WE have endeavoured to describe the general features of the average Highland parish of our own times. There are a few peculiarities long associated with the Highlands—such as witchcraft, second-sight, and certain other superstitious beliefs—to which some may think a distinct chapter should have been allotted. Such beliefs, however, are all but vanished, being very much scared by railways, newspapers, and schools, not to speak of the influence of the pulpit, though this latter has not always been so helpful as might be wished. As, however, such beliefs widely prevailed until within a recent period, and as isolated traces of them may yet exist, a few general remarks on the subject may suitably occupy a part of this concluding chapter.

Reputed witches and uncanny ones of that ilk,

that "took away" the milk, as was alleged, from cows, and that dealt in other mischievous practices, were by no means rare in the Highlands about twenty years ago. We remember some score years ago having seen a representative of the hated sisterhood. She was old, and had a wrinkled and somewhat sable face,—all which features, of course, are ordinarily considered requisites in a witch. She invariably carried about with her a small tin pail, and it was in this pail the appliances for her alleged diabolical artifices were believed to reside. She was peculiar among witches because of the pail. Other witches went about without a pail, and were not supposed to be engaged in evil-doing beyond the *pale* of their homes, whereas the *pail* witch was believed to be capable of doing injury anywhere *with the pail.* Schoolboys half trembled at the sight of her when she came from her home in the hills to the little village; and certain owners of cattle no sooner saw her than they deputed a special messenger to go to look after the cows, lest by her odious charms, as was alleged, she might "take away," or take the *virtue* from, the milk. In such houses as she honoured with a visit it was thought prudent to be kind to her; for—so thought those that made her peace-offerings—who knew what she might do to man or beast, or both? She and her pail have disappeared some dozen years ago, and though she had several rival witches in her day in her neighbourhood, it will to-day be difficult in the same district to find even one successor.

We also remember having frequently seen in a Highland parish some twenty years ago an old man, one of several believed in the district to possess second-sight. He said that he "saw" funerals weeks before the event; and it was alleged that at church, and other gatherings, he at times "saw" on some one or other a shroud!—a sure sign that the person was soon to die, the nearness of the event being in proportion to the extent of the body covered by the shroud. If to the waist, a month or two might elapse, but if to the neck, a few days only, while if reaching the head, an early sudden death might be expected. Others again, not however persons credited with second-sight, alleged that they saw and heard premonitions of death,— such as hearing noises and seeing lights in a joiner's shop when it was known the workmen were away— these sounds and lights being taken as a proof that a coffin would very soon be made in the joiner's workshop. Some years ago we heard a somewhat intelligent shopkeeper in a Highland parish gravely saying that one afternoon in his shop he saw a bundle of white cotton moving voluntarily on a shelf and unfold itself along the floor! which automatic exercise he explained by saying that part of the cotton was soon after used as a shroud.

A remarkably tenacious superstition is the belief in "the seventh son" being able to cure scrofula. We knew some dozen years ago two cases where this, so to speak, inherited royal-touch cure was being tried. In one of the cases the seventh son, called the "doctor" by the other members of the family, and a very smart little fellow, was so young that he had to be carried a part of the way to the residence of his patient. The "doctor" is to-day a big boy—a young man, indeed—and right heartily does he laugh at the elaborate farce in which he was wont in early life to play so important a part. In some districts there is no small credence given to the allegation that certain days are unlucky, and many persons consider it unlucky to find a pin or meet a toad on the road; and there are instances of people avoiding meeting certain persons, whom to meet they consider unlucky. These and suchlike time-honoured beliefs and customs, we repeat, are fading. A few yet believe in them, encouraged in some instances by remarkable coincidences and the wish to believe; but the growing doubt regarding them among grown-up people generally, and the utter disbelief in them, as a rule, among the young and the educated, clearly prove these beliefs and customs must soon altogether yield to the progress of to-day.

Some may have desiderated in these pages more special attention to the subject of education and schools. This is unnecessary. The matter has been incidentally referred to in one or two portions of the book, and such other features as are special and important may be briefly told.

Gaelic schools, once common in the Highlands, are now exceeding rare. Ten years ago we visited a Gaelic school taught by an intelligent old man,— who, by the way, expressed but slender faith in the necessity of his special work. The district is a populous one, containing some three hundred inhabitants, but there were only some half-dozen pupils. To-day there is not one pupil. A few hundred yards from where the Gaelic school used to be there is a large Board school, with two teachers, but Gaelic is not taught; and it is worth mentioning, that while thirty years ago the great majority of teachers in the Highlands could speak Gaelic, to-day very many are unable to speak it.

The changes brought about in educational matters by the Act of 1872 are, as yet, not marked. Many parishes have more schools, but the compulsory clause does not in every place show improved attendance. In the matter of religious instruction in schools, "use and wont" may be said to be universally required, School Boards usually deputing the clergy to inquire into the manner in which this important matter is attended to.

Education, generally speaking, is undoubtedly making rapid strides in the Highlands, and did so likewise under the old parochial system, which, as a rule, worked admirably in the Northern Highlands. Thirty years ago, in a Highland parish of say fourteen hundred inhabitants, it would have been easy enough to find three hundred, or nearly one-fourth, unable to read or write, while in a similar parish to-day it will be difficult to find sixty persons thus uneducated. No doubt, just like other people, some Highlanders that take up the pen make at times a slightly remarkable figure with it. During the taking of the census of 1871, a West Highland crofter, 46 years old, wrote down his age at 406, the adding of *nothing*, strange to say, giving him an antediluvian venerableness. But since the last census there has been a marked progress educationally among the crofter population, so that in future there will be less likelihood of a similarly inaccurate ciphering taking place.

It may be thought by some that a special chapter should have been devoted to an account of the general character of the residents in a Highland parish of to-day. This would have been advisable, and even necessary, were the character-peculiarities of such residents numerous or marked. Such peculiarities of character and disposition as were associated with the Highlander when the Highlands were remote have very much faded, along with the individuality of the Highlander of that period—an individuality now very much, because of the growing communication with the larger world outside his native hills and glens, merged in the national life and character. Bravery, hardihood, and endurance yet characterise the better type of Highlander; but, happily, the isolation and local misunderstandings, to put the latter mildly, that so often long ago called forth these qualities in uninviting fields, are altogether, in the case of the latter, and all but in the case of the former, gone. The perseverance and determination implied in the qualities mentioned are to no small extent observable to-day in more peaceful walks of life; and it is well known that, because of these two latter features, Highlanders going to push their fortune in southern towns and in foreign lands are often especially successful. As to other features of character little need be said. For a long time Highlanders were believed by many to be a simple-minded if not guileless people; while others in recent times speak of them in quite a different strain. Each estimate, very probably, is partial truth. We suppose that, so far as guile and guilelessness are concerned, Highlanders are very much like their fellow-creatures the whole world over, and neither better than they ought to be, nor perhaps so bad as they themselves allege of each other,—so that it is unnecessary to discuss the matter. To-day we occasionally meet a veritable Nathanael in a Highland parish; but though, as a class, as genuine very probably as their neighbours, to call them guileless as a people would be to say what few, if any, of themselves believe. It is common enough in a Highland parish of to-day to hear such expressions among the natives as "the people are getting much sharper and *smairter* like than they were before;" and such sharpness and smartness, though referred to as evidence of progress, are mentioned in a tone and manner calculated to convey the impression that there is no wish or reason to claim for the people a prevailing guilelessness.

It may be worth noticing, also, that some who can compare the Highlands past and of to-day declare that the people are less social to-day, less kindly interested, indeed, in each other's welfare. It would be foreign to our purpose to discuss this matter at length. It may be observed, however, that the fact of the people to-day being busier, and competition greater, may partly explain the change, if change there be. We do not think that, beyond what might be thus accounted for, there is any marked absence of the sort of kindliness indicated; and even should the people seem to be less kindly, which we fear is true of some, to some extent there is a real widening of healthful sympathies, brought about by the changes that have diminished what was a merely local, and often only an apparent, attachment. Some people, more prejudiced than enlightened, allege that at the period of the Secession of 1843 from the Church of Scotland, practical Christianity was at a low ebb in the Highlands; but the general character of the Highlanders at present in the matter of purity and truthfulness cannot be said to prove that any moral improvement has taken place in the Highlands as the result of that Secession; nor, besides, is it easy to avoid the conclusion that if pulpit utterances in a certain quarter had been less devoid of Christian charity, a greater measure of friendliness, and consequently of straightforwardness, might to-day characterise the people generally. That there are kindly and straightforward ones among Highlanders, and, relatively, as many as among other people, we rejoice to believe; and notwithstanding that some of themselves regettingly allege that "the people are no what they were,"—that, in other words, deterioration in general character has taken place, and especially in the matter of truthfulness and purity of life—we believe that under intelligent, manly leadership in matters religious, and with definite encouragement towards self-improvement and the bettering of their general circumstances, Highlanders, as many of them have already done, would, as much at least as other people, reflect credit on themselves, and constitute no small help to the promotion of the national welfare.

And now we have done. With reference to any subject which may have been either omitted or only slightly referred to, it will, we think, be found such matter is either not peculiar to Highland parishes, or if peculiar, will soon cease to be so. We trust we have succeeded in describing the actual circumstances of the average Highland parish of to-day, and it has been our endeavour to make the description representative, with the view of including the Highlands generally, and, more especially, the rural districts.

Should any enthusiastic Highlander have desiderated more detailed reference to the heroic deeds in which Highlanders in days of yore took part, or have liked less confident forecasting as to the prospects of Gaelic as a spoken language, and more exhaustive treatment of beliefs and customs long associated with the Highlands, we must remind such enthusiastic one that, while sympathising with him in what is virtually a fond patriotic remembering of other days, our aim has been to describe a Highland parish of *to-day*.

THE END.

CATALOGUE

OF

MESSRS BLACKWOOD & SONS' PUBLICATIONS.

PHILOSOPHICAL CLASSICS FOR ENGLISH READERS

EDITED BY WILLIAM KNIGHT, LL.D.,
Professor of Moral Philosophy in the University of St Andrews.

In crown 8vo Volumes, with Portraits, price 3s. 6d.

Now Ready.

I. **Descartes.** By Professor MAHAFFY, Dublin.
II. **Butler.** By Rev. W. L. COLLINS, M.A.
III. **Berkeley.** By Professor FRASER, Edinburgh.

The Volumes in preparation are—

IV. FICHTE. By Prof. Adamson, Owen's College, Manchester. [*Immediately.*]
HAMILTON. By Professor Veitch, Glasgow.
HUME. By the Editor.
BACON. By Professor Nichol, Glasgow.
HEGEL. By Professor Edward Caird, Glasgow.

HOBBES. By Professor Croom Robertson, London.
KANT. By William Wallace, Merton College, Oxford.
SPINOZA. By Dr Martineau, Principal of Manchester New College.
VICO. By Professor Flint, Edinburgh.

IN COURSE OF PUBLICATION.

FOREIGN CLASSICS FOR ENGLISH READERS.

EDITED BY MRS OLIPHANT.

In Crown 8vo, 2s. 6d.

The Volumes published are—

DANTE. By the Editor.
VOLTAIRE. By Major-General Sir E. B. Hamley, K.C.M.G.
PASCAL. By Principal Tulloch.
PETRARCH. By Henry Reeve, C.B.
GOETHE. By A. Hayward, Q.C.
MOLIÈRE. By the Editor and F. Tarver, M.A.

MONTAIGNE. By Rev. W. Lucas Collins, M.A.
RABELAIS. By Walter Besant, M.A.
CALDERON. By E. J. Hasell.
SAINT SIMON. By Clifton W. Collins, M.A.
CERVANTES. By the Editor.
CORNEILLE AND RACINE. By Henry M. Trollope.

In preparation—

MADAME DE SÉVIGNÉ. By Miss Thackeray.—SCHILLER. By James Sime, Author of 'Life of Lessing.'—ROUSSEAU. By Henry Graham.—LA FONTAINE. By Rev. W. Lucas Collins, M.A.

Now Complete.

ANCIENT CLASSICS FOR ENGLISH READERS.

EDITED BY THE REV. W. LUCAS COLLINS, M.A.

Complete in 28 Vols. crown 8vo, cloth, price 2s. 6d. each. And may also be had in 14 Volumes, strongly and neatly bound, with calf or vellum back, £3, 10s.

Saturday Review.—"It is difficult to estimate too highly the value of such a series as this in giving 'English readers' an insight, exact as far as it goes, into those olden times which are so remote and yet to many of us so close."

CATALOGUE

OF

MESSRS BLACKWOOD & SONS' PUBLICATIONS.

ALISON. History of Europe. By Sir ARCHIBALD ALISON, Bart., D.C.L.

1. From the Commencement of the French Revolution to the Battle of Waterloo.
   LIBRARY EDITION, 14 vols., with Portraits. Demy 8vo, £10, 10s.
   ANOTHER EDITION, in 20 vols. crown 8vo, £6.
   PEOPLE'S EDITION, 13 vols. crown 8vo, £2, 11s.

2. Continuation to the Accession of Louis Napoleon.
   LIBRARY EDITION, 8 vols. 8vo, £6, 7s. 6d.
   PEOPLE'S EDITION, 8 vols. crown 8vo, 34s.

3. Epitome of Alison's History of Europe. Twenty-eighth Thousand, 7s. 6d.

4. Atlas to Alison's History of Europe. By A. Keith Johnston.
   LIBRARY EDITION, demy 4to, £3, 3s.
   PEOPLE'S EDITION, 31s. 6d.

—— Life of John Duke of Marlborough. With some Account of his Contemporaries, and of the War of the Succession. Third Edition, 2 vols. 8vo. Portraits and Maps, 30s.

—— Essays: Historical, Political, and Miscellaneous. 3 vols. demy 8vo, 45s.

—— Lives of Lord Castlereagh and Sir Charles Stewart, Second and Third Marquesses of Londonderry. From the Original Papers of the Family. 3 vols. 8vo, £2, 2s.

—— Principles of the Criminal Law of Scotland. 8vo, 18s.

—— Practice of the Criminal Law of Scotland. 8vo, cloth boards, 18s.

—— The Principles of Population, and their Connection with Human Happiness. 2 vols. 8vo, 30s.

ALISON. On the Management of the Poor in Scotland, and its Effects on the Health of the Great Towns. By WILLIAM PULTENEY ALISON, M.D. Crown 8vo, 5s. 6d.

ADAMS. Great Campaigns. A Succinct Account of the Principal Military Operations which have taken place in Europe from 1796 to 1870. By Major C. ADAMS, Professor of Military History at the Staff College. Edited by Captain C. COOPER KING, R.M. Artillery, Instructor of Tactics, Royal Military College. 8vo, with Maps. 16s.

AIRD. Poetical Works of Thomas Aird. Fifth Edition, with Memoir of the Author by the Rev. JARDINE WALLACE, and Portrait. Crown 8vo, 7s 6d.

—— The Old Bachelor in the Old Scottish Village. Fcap. 8vo, 4s.

ALEXANDER. Moral Causation; or, Notes on Mr Mill's Notes to the Chapter on "Freedom" in the Third Edition of his 'Examination of Sir William Hamilton's Philosophy.' By PATRICK PROCTOR ALEXANDER, M A., Author of 'Mill and Carlyle,' &c. Second Edition, revised and extended. Crown 8vo, 6s.

ALLARDYCE. The City of Sunshine. By ALEXANDER ALLARDYCE. Three vols. post 8vo, £1. 5s. 6d.

ANCIENT CLASSICS FOR ENGLISH READERS. Edited by Rev. W. LUCAS COLLINS, M.A. Complete in 28 vols., cloth, 2s. 6d. each; or in 14 vols., tastefully bound with calf or vellum back, £3, 10s.

Contents of the Series.

HOMER: THE ILIAD. By the Editor.
HOMER: THE ODYSSEY. By the Editor.
HERODOTUS. By George C. Swayne, M.A.
XENOPHON. By Sir Alexander Grant, Bart., LL.D.
EURIPIDES. By W. B. Donne.
ARISTOPHANES. By the Editor.
PLATO. By Clifton W. Collins, M.A.
LUCIAN. By the Editor.
ÆSCHYLUS. By the Right Rev. the Bishop of Colombo.
SOPHOCLES. By Clifton W. Collins, M.A.
HESIOD AND THEOGNIS. By the Rev. J. Davies, M.A.
GREEK ANTHOLOGY. By Lord Neaves.
VIRGIL. By the Editor.
HORACE. By Sir Theodore Martin, K.C.B.
JUVENAL. By Edward Walford, M.A.

PLAUTUS AND TERENCE. By the Editor.
THE COMMENTARIES OF CÆSAR. By Anthony Trollope.
TACITUS By W. B. Donne.
CICERO. By the Editor.
PLINY'S LETTERS. By the Rev. Alfred Church, M.A., and the Rev. W. J. Brodribb, M.A.
LIVY. By the Editor.
OVID. By the Rev. A. Church, M.A.
CATULLUS, TIBULLUS, AND PROPERTIUS. By the Rev. Jas. Davies, M.A
DEMOSTHENES. By the Rev. W. J. Brodribb, M.A.
ARISTOTLE. By Sir Alexander Grant, Bart., LL.D.
THUCYDIDES. By the Editor.
LUCRETIUS. By W H. Mallock. M.A
PINDAR. By the Rev. F. D. Morice, M. A.

AYLWARD. The Transvaal of To-day: War, Witchcraft, Sports, and Spoils in South Africa. By ALFRED AYLWARD, Commandant, Transvaal Republic; Captain (late) Lydenberg Volunteer Corps. Second Edition. Crown 8vo, with a Map, 6s.

AYTOUN. Lays of the Scottish Cavaliers, and other Poems. By W. EDMONDSTOUNE AYTOUN, D.C.L., Professor of Rhetoric and Belles-Lettres in the University of Edinburgh. Twenty-seventh Edition. Fcap. 8vo, 7s. 6d.

—— An Illustrated Edition of the Lays of the Scottish Cavaliers. From designs by Sir NOEL PATON. Small 4to, 21s., in gilt cloth.

—— Bothwell: a Poem. Third Edition. Fcap., 7s. 6d.

—— Firmilian; or, The Student of Badajoz. A Spasmodic Tragedy. Fcap., 5s.

—— Poems and Ballads of Goethe. Translated by Professor AYTOUN and Sir THEODORE MARTIN, K.C.B. Third Edition. Fcap., 6s.

—— Bon Gaultier's Book of Ballads. By the SAME. Thirteenth Edition. With Illustrations by Doyle, Leech, and Crowquill. Post 8vo, gilt edges, 8s. 6d.

—— The Ballads of Scotland. Edited by Professor AYTOUN. Fourth Edition. 2 vols. fcap. 8vo, 12s.

—— Memoir of William E. Aytoun, D.C.L. By Sir THEODORE MARTIN, K.C.B. With Portrait. Post 8vo, 12s.

BAGOT. The Art of Poetry of Horace. Free and Explanatory Translations in Prose and Verse. By the Very Rev. DANIEL BAGOT, D. D. Third Edition, Revised, printed on *papier vergé*, square 8vo, 5s.

BAIRD LECTURES. The Mysteries of Christianity. By T. J. CRAWFORD, D.D., F.R.S.E., Professor of Divinity in the University of Edinburgh, &c. Being the Baird Lecture for 1874. Crown 8vo, 7s. 6d.

―――― Endowed Territorial Work: Its Supreme Importance to the Church and Country. By WILLIAM SMITH, D.D., Minister of North Leith. Being the Baird Lecture for 1875. Crown 8vo, 6s.

―――― Theism. By ROBERT FLINT, D.D., LL.D., Professor of Divinity in the University of Edinburgh. Being the Baird Lecture for 1876. Third Edition. Crown 8vo, 7s. 6d.

―――― Anti-Theistic Theories. By the SAME. Being the Baird Lecture for 1877. Second Edition. Crown 8vo, 10s. 6d.

BATTLE OF DORKING. Reminiscences of a Volunteer. From 'Blackwood's Magazine.' Second Hundredth Thousand. 6d.

BY THE SAME AUTHOR.

The Dilemma. Cheap Edition. Crown 8vo, 6s.

A True Reformer. 3 vols. crown 8vo, £1, 5s. 6d.

BESANT. Readings from Rabelais. By WALTER BESANT, M.A. In one volume, post 8vo. [In the press.

BLACKIE. Lays and Legends of Ancient Greece. By JOHN STUART BLACKIE, Professor of Greek in the University of Edinburgh. Second Edition. Fcap. 8vo. 5s.

BLACKWOOD'S MAGAZINE, from Commencement in 1817 to June 1880. Nos. 1 to 776, forming 127 Volumes.

―――― Index to Blackwood's Magazine. Vols. 1 to 50. 8vo, 15s.

―――― Tales from Blackwood. Forming Twelve Volumes of Interesting and Amusing Railway Reading. Price One Shilling each in Paper Cover. Sold separately at all Railway Bookstalls.

They may also be had bound in cloth, 18s., and in half calf, richly gilt, 30s. or 12 volumes in 6, half Roxburghe, 21s., and half red morocco, 28s.

―――― Tales from Blackwood. New Series. Complete in Twenty-four Shilling Parts. Handsomely bound in 12 vols., cloth, 30s. In leather back, Roxburghe style, 37s. 6d. In half calf, gilt, 52s. 6d. In half morocco, 55s.

―――― Standard Novels. Uniform in size and legibly Printed. Each Novel complete in one volume.

Florin Series, Illustrated Boards.

TOM CRINGLE'S LOG. By Michael Scott.
THE CRUISE OF THE MIDGE. By the Same.
CYRIL THORNTON. By Captain Hamilton.
ANNALS OF THE PARISH. By John Galt.
THE PROVOST, &c. By John Galt.
SIR ANDREW WYLIE. By John Galt.
THE ENTAIL. By John Galt.
MISS MOLLY. By Beatrice May Butt.
REGINALD DALTON. By J. G. Lockhart.
PEN OWEN. By Dean Hook.
ADAM BLAIR. By J. G. Lockhart.
LADY LEE'S WIDOWHOOD. By General Sir E. B. Hamley.
SALEM CHAPEL. By Mrs Oliphant.
THE PERPETUAL CURATE. By Mrs Oliphant.
MISS MARJORIBANKS. By Mrs Oliphant.
JOHN: A Love Story. By Mrs Oliphant.

Or in Cloth Boards, 2s. 6d.

Shilling Series, Illustrated Cover.

THE RECTOR, and THE DOCTOR'S FAMILY. By Mrs Oliphant.
THE LIFE OF MANSIE WAUCH. By D. M. Moir.
PENINSULAR SCENES AND SKETCHES. By F. Hardman.
SIR FRIZZLE PUMPKIN, NIGHTS AT MESS, &c.
THE SUBALTERN.
LIFE IN THE FAR WEST. By G. F. Ruxton.
VALERIUS: A Roman Story. By J. G. Lockhart.

Or in Cloth Boards, 1s. 6d.

BLACKMORE. The Maid of Sker. By R. D. BLACKMORE, Author of 'Lorna Doone,' &c. Seventh Edition. Crown 8vo, 7s. 6d.

BOSCOBEL TRACTS. Relating to the Escape of Charles the Second after the Battle of Worcester, and his subsequent Adventures. Edited by J. HUGHES, Esq., A.M. A New Edition, with additional Notes and Illustrations, including Communications from the Rev. R. H. BARHAM, Author of the 'Ingoldsby Legends.' 8vo, with Engravings, 16s.

BRACKENBURY. A Narrative of the Ashanti War. Prepared from the official documents, by permission of Major-General Sir Garnet Wolseley, K.C.B., K.C.M.G. By Major H. BRACKENBURY, R.A., Assistant Military Secretary to Sir Garnet Wolseley. With Maps from the latest Surveys made by the Staff of the Expedition. 2 vols. 8vo, 25s.

BROOKE, Life of Sir James, Rajah of Sarāwak. From his Personal Papers and Correspondence. By SPENSER ST JOHN, H.M.'s Minister-Resident and Consul-General Peruvian Republic; formerly Secretary to the Rajah. With Portrait and a Map. Post 8vo, 12s. 6d.

BROUGHAM. Memoirs of the Life and Times of Henry Lord Brougham. Written by HIMSELF. 3 vols. 8vo, £2, 8s. The Volumes are sold separately, price 16s. each.

BROWN. The Forester: A Practical Treatise on the Planting, Rearing, and General Management of Forest-trees. By JAMES BROWN, Wood-Surveyor and Nurseryman. Fifth Edition, revised and enlarged. Royal 8vo, with Engravings. [In the press.

BROWN. The Ethics of George Eliot's Works. By JOHN CROMBIE BROWN. Third Edition. Crown 8vo, 2s. 6d.

BROWN. A Manual of Botany, Anatomical and Physiological. For the Use of Students. By ROBERT BROWN, M.A., Ph.D., F.L.S., F.R.G.S. Crown 8vo, with numerous Illustrations, 12s. 6d.

BROWN. Book of the Landed Estate. Containing Directions for the Management and Development of the Resources of Landed Property. By ROBERT E. BROWN, Factor and Estate Agent. Large 8vo, with Illustrations, 21s.

BUCHAN. Introductory Text-Book of Meteorology. By ALEXANDER BUCHAN, M.A., F.R.S.E., Secretary of the Scottish Meteorological Society, &c. Crown 8vo, with 8 Coloured Charts and other Engravings, pp. 218. 4s. 6d.

BURBIDGE. Domestic Floriculture, Window Gardening, and Floral Decorations. Being practical directions for the Propagation, Culture, and Arrangement of Plants and Flowers as Domestic Ornaments. By F. W. BURBIDGE. Second Edition. Crown 8vo, with numerous Illustrations, 7s. 6d.

—— Cultivated Plants: Their Propagation and Improvement. Including Natural and Artificial Hybridisation, Raising from Seed, Cuttings, and Layers, Grafting and Budding, as applied to the Families and Genera in Cultivation. Crown 8vo, with numerous Illustrations, 12s. 6d.

BURN. Handbook of the Mechanical Arts Concerned in the Construction and Arrangement of Dwelling-Houses and other Buildings; with Practical Hints on Road-making and the Enclosing of Land. By ROBERT SCOTT BURN, Engineer. Second Edition. Crown 8vo, 6s. 6d.

BUTE. The Roman Breviary: Reformed by Order of the Holy Œcumenical Council of Trent; Published by Order of Pope St Pius V.; and Revised by Clement VIII. and Urban VIII.; together with the Offices since granted. Translated out of Latin into English by JOHN, Marquess of Bute, K.T. In 2 vols. crown 8vo, cloth boards, edges uncut. £2, 2s.

BUTT. Miss Molly. By BEATRICE MAY BUTT. Cheap Edition, 2s.

—— Delicia. By the Author of 'Miss Molly.' Fourth Edition. Crown 8vo, 7s. 6d.

BURTON. The History of Scotland: From Agricola's Invasion to the Extinction of the last Jacobite Insurrection. By JOHN HILL BURTON, D.C.L., Historiographer-Royal for Scotland. New and Enlarged Edition, 8 vols., and Index. Crown 8vo, £3, 3s.

BURTON. History of the British Empire during the Reign of
Queen Anne. In 3 vols. 8vo. 36s.
—— The Cairngorm Mountains. Crown 8vo, 3s. 6d.
CAIRD. Sermons. By JOHN CAIRD, D.D., Principal of the University of Glasgow. Fourteenth Thousand. Fcap. 8vo, 5s.
—— Religion in Common Life. A Sermon preached in Crathie Church, October 14, 1855, before Her Majesty the Queen and Prince Albert. Published by Her Majesty's Command. Price One Shilling. Cheap Edition, 3d.
CAMPBELL, Life of Colin, Lord Clyde. *See* General SHADWELL, at page 20.
CARLYLE. Autobiography of the Rev. Dr Alexander Carlyle, Minister of Inveresk. Containing Memorials of the Men and Events of his Time. Edited by JOHN HILL BURTON. 8vo. Third Edition, with Portrait, 14s.
CAUVIN. A Treasury of the English and German Languages. Compiled from the best Authors and Lexicographers in both Languages. Adapted to the Use of Schools, Students, Travellers, and Men of Business; and forming a Companion to all German-English Dictionaries. By JOSEPH CAUVIN, LL.D. & Ph.D., of the University of Göttingen, &c. Crown 8vo, 7s. 6d.
CHARTERIS. Canonicity; or, Early Testimonies to the Existence and Use of the Books of the New Testament. Based on Kirchhoffer's 'Quellensammlung.' Edited by A. H. CHARTERIS, D.D., Professor of Biblical Criticism in the University of Edinburgh. 8vo, 18s.
—— Life of the Rev. James Robertson, D.D., F.R.S.E., Professor of Divinity and Ecclesiastical History in the University of Edinburgh. By Professor CHARTERIS. With Portrait. 8vo. 10s. 6d.
CHETWYND. Life in a German Village. By the Hon. Mrs HENRY WEYLAND CHETWYND, Author of 'Neighbours and Friends,' 'Janie, 'Mdlle. d'Estanville,' &c. &c. Second Edition. Crown 8vo, 7s. 6d.
CHEVELEY NOVELS, THE.
  I. A MODERN MINISTER. 2 vols. bound in cloth, with Twenty-six Illustrations. 17s.
  II. SAUL WEIR. 2 vols. bound in cloth. With Twelve Illustrations by F. Barnard. 16s.
CHIROL. 'Twixt Greek and Turk. By M. VALENTINE CHIROL. In one volume, post 8vo. With Frontispiece and Map. [*In the press.*
CHURCH SERVICE SOCIETY. A Book of Common Order: Being Forms of Worship issued by the Church Service Society. Fourth Edition, 5s.
COLQUHOUN. The Moor and the Loch. Containing Minute Instructions in all Highland Sports, with Wanderings over Crag and Corrie, Flood and Fell. By JOHN COLQUHOUN. Fifth Edition, greatly enlarged. With Illustrations. 2 vols. post 8vo, 26s.
COTTERILL. The Genesis of the Church. By the Right. Rev. HENRY COTTERILL, D.D., Bishop of Edinburgh. Demy 8vo, 16s.
CRANSTOUN. The Elegies of Albius Tibullus. Translated into English Verse, with Life of the Poet, and Illustrative Notes. By JAMES CRANSTOUN, LL.D., Author of a Translation of 'Catullus.' Crown 8vo, 6s. 6d.
—— The Elegies of Sextus Propertius. Translated into English Verse, with Life of the Poet, and Illustrative Notes. Crown 8vo, 7s. 6d.
CRAWFORD. The Doctrine of Holy Scripture respecting the Atonement. By the late THOMAS J. CRAWFORD, D.D., Professor of Divinity in the University of Edinburgh. Third Edition. 8vo, 12s.

CRAWFORD. The Fatherhood of God, Considered in its General and Special Aspects, and particularly in relation to the Atonement, with a Review of Recent Speculations on the Subject. Third Edition, Revised and Enlarged. 8vo, 9s.

—— The Preaching of the Cross, and other Sermons. 8vo, 7s. 6d.

—— The Mysteries of Christianity; being the Baird Lecture for 1874. Crown 8vo, 7s. 6d

CROSSE. Round about the Carpathians. By ANDREW F. CROSSE, F.C.S. 8vo, with Map of the Author's route, price 12s. 6d.

DESCARTES. The Method, Meditations, and Principles of Philosophy of Descartes. Translated from the Original French and Latin. With a New Introductory Essay, Historical and Critical, on the Cartesian Philosophy. By JOHN VEITCH, LL.D., Professor of Logic and Rhetoric in the University of Glasgow. A New Edition, being the Eighth. Price 6s. 6d.

DICKSON. Japan; being a Sketch of the History, Government, and Officers of the Empire. By WALTER DICKSON. 8vo, 15s.

DU CANE. The Odyssey of Homer, Books I.-XII. Translated into English Verse. By Sir CHARLES DU CANE, K.C.M.G. 8vo, 10s. 6d.

EAGLES. Essays. By the Rev. JOHN EAGLES, A.M. Oxon. Originally published in 'Blackwood's Magazine.' Post 8vo, 10s. 6d.

—— The Sketcher. Originally published in 'Blackwood's Magazine.' Post 8vo, 10s. 6d

ELIOT. Impressions of Theophrastus Such. By GEORGE ELIOT. Fourth Edition. Post 8vo, 10s. 6d. New and cheaper Edition. Crown 8vo, 5s.

—— Adam Bede. Illustrated Edition. 3s. 6d., cloth.

—— The Mill on the Floss. Illustrated Edition. 3s. 6d., cloth.

—— Scenes of Clerical Life. Illustrated Edition. 3s., cloth.

—— Silas Marner: The Weaver of Raveloe. Illustrated Edition. 2s. 6d., cloth

—— Felix Holt, the Radical. Illustrated Edition. 3s. 6d., cloth.

—— Romola. With Vignette. 3s. 6d., cloth.

—— Middlemarch. Crown 8vo, 7s. 6d.

—— Daniel Deronda. Crown 8vo, 7s. 6d.

—— Works of George Eliot (Cabinet Edition). Complete and Uniform Edition, handsomely printed in a new type, 20 volumes, crown 8vo price £5. The Volumes are also sold separately, price 5s. each, viz.:—
Romola. 2 vols.—Silas Marner, The Lifted Veil, Brother Jacob. 1 vol.—Adam Bede. 2 vols.—Scenes of Clerical Life. 2 vols.—The Mill on the Floss. 2 vols.—Felix Holt 2 vols.—Middlemarch. 3 vols.—Daniel Deronda. 3 vols.—The Spanish Gypsy. 1 vol.—Jubal, and other Poems, Old and New. 1 vol.—Theophrastus Such. 1 vol.

—— The Spanish Gypsy. Seventh Edition. Crown 8vo, 7s. 6d., cloth.

—— The Legend of Jubal, and other Poems. New Edition. Fcap. 8vo, 5s., cloth.

—— Wise, Witty, and Tender Sayings, in Prose and Verse. Selected from the Works of GEORGE ELIOT. Fifth Edition. Fcap. 8vo, 6s.

—— The George Eliot Birthday Book. Printed on fine paper, with red border, and handsomely bound in cloth, gilt. Fcap. 8vo, cloth, 3s. 6d. And in French morocco or Russia, 5s.

ESSAYS ON SOCIAL SUBJECTS. Originally published in the 'Saturday Review.' A New Edition. First and Second Series. 2 vols. crown 8vo, 6s. each.

EWALD. The Crown and its Advisers; or, Queen, Ministers, Lords, and Commons. By ALEXANDER CHARLES EWALD, F.S.A. Crown 8vo, 5s.

FERRIER. Philosophical Works of the late James F. Ferrier, B.A. Oxon., Professor of Moral Philosophy and Political Economy, St Andrews. New Edition. Edited by Sir ALEX. GRANT, Bart., D.C.L., and Professor LUSHINGTON. 3 vols. crown 8vo, 34s. 6d.

———— Institutes of Metaphysic. Third Edition. 10s. 6d.

———— Lectures on the Early Greek Philosophy. Third Edition. 10s. 6d.

———— Philosophical Remains, including the Lectures on Early Greek Philosophy. 2 vols., 24s.

FERRIER. George Eliot and Judaism. An Attempt to appreciate 'Daniel Deronda.' By Professor DAVID KAUFMANN, of the Jewish Theological Seminary, Buda-Pesth. Translated from the German by J. W. FERRIER. Second Edition. Crown 8vo, 2s. 6d.

FINLAY. History of Greece under Foreign Domination. By the late GEORGE FINLAY, LL.D., Athens. 6 vols. 8vo—viz.:

Greece under the Romans. B.C. 146 to A.D. 717. · A Historical View of the Condition of the Greek Nation from its Conquest by the Romans until the Extinction of the Roman Power in the East. Second Edition, 16s.

History of the Byzantine Empire. A.D. 716 to 1204; and of the Greek Empire of Nicæa and Constantinople, A.D. 1204 to 1453. 2 vols., £1, 7s. 6d.

Greece under Othoman and Venetian Domination. A.D. 1453 to 1821. 10s. 6d.

History of the Greek Revolution of 1830. 2 vols. 8vo, £1, 4s.

FLINT. The Philosophy of History in Europe. Vol. I., containing the History of that Philosophy in France and Germany. By ROBERT FLINT, D.D., LL.D., Professor of Divinity, University of Edinburgh. 8vo, 15s.

———— Theism. Being the Baird Lecture for 1876. Third Edition. Crown 8vo, 7s. 6d.

———— Anti-Theistic Theories. Being the Baird Lecture for 1877. Second Edition. Crown 8vo, 10s. 6d.

FORBES. The Campaign of Garibaldi in the Two Sicilies: A Personal Narrative. By CHARLES STUART FORBES, Commander, R.N. Post 8vo, with Portraits, 12s.

FOREIGN CLASSICS FOR ENGLISH READERS. Edited by Mrs OLIPHANT. Price 2s. 6d.

Now published:—I. DANTE. By the Editor.—II. VOLTAIRE. By Major-General Sir E. B. Hamley.—III. PASCAL. By Principal Tulloch.—IV. PETRARCH. By Henry Reeve, C.B.—V. GOETHE. By A. Hayward, Q.C.—VI. MOLIÈRE. By the Editor and F. Tarver, M.A.—VII. MONTAIGNE. By Rev. W. L. Collins, M.A.—VIII. RABELAIS. By Walter Besant, M.A.—IX. CALDERON. By E. J. Hasell.—X. SAINT SIMON. By Clifton W. Collins, M.A.—XI. CERVANTES. By the Editor.—XII. CORNEILLE AND RACINE. By Henry M. Trollope.

In preparation:—MADAME DE SÉVIGNÉ. By Miss Thackeray.—SCHILLER. By James Sime, Author of 'Life of Lessing.'—ROUSSEAU. By Henry Graham.—LA FONTAINE. By Rev. W. L. Collins, M.A.

FRASER. Handy Book of Ornamental Conifers, and of Rhododendrons and other American Flowering Shrubs, suitable for the Climate and Soils of Britain. With descriptions of the best kinds, and containing Useful Hints for their successful Cultivation. By HUGH FRASER, Fellow of the Botanical Society of Edinburgh. Crown 8vo, 6s.

GALT. Annals of the Parish. By JOHN GALT. Fcap. 8vo, 2s.

―――― The Provost. Fcap. 8vo, 2s.

―――― Sir Andrew Wylie. Fcap. 8vo, 2s.

―――― The Entail; or, The Laird of Grippy. Fcap. 8vo, 2s.

GARDENER, THE: A Magazine of Horticulture and Floriculture. Edited by DAVID THOMSON, Author of 'The Handy Book of the Flower-Garden,' &c.; Assisted by a Staff of the best practical Writers. Published Monthly, 6d

GENERAL ASSEMBLY OF THE CHURCH OF SCOTLAND.
―――― Family Prayers. Authorised by the General Assembly of the Church of Scotland. A New Edition, crown 8vo, in large type, 4s. 6d. Another Edition, crown 8vo, 2s.

―――― Prayers for Social and Family Worship. For the Use of Soldiers, Sailors, Colonists, and Sojourners in India, and other Persons, at home and abroad, who are deprived of the ordinary services of a Christian Ministry. Cheap Edition, 1s. 6d.

―――― The Scottish Hymnal. Hymns for Public Worship. Published for Use in Churches by Authority of the General Assembly. Various sizes—viz.: 1. Large type, for pulpit use, cloth, 3s. 6d. 2. Longprimer type, cloth, red edges, 1s. 6d.; French morocco, 2s. 6d.; calf, 6s. 3. Bourgeois type, cloth, red edges, 1s.; French morocco, 2s. 4. Minion type, limp cloth, 6d.; French morocco, 1s. 6d. 5. School Edition, in paper cover, 2d. 6. Children's Hymnal, paper cover, 1d. No. 2, bound with the Psalms and Paraphrases, cloth, 3s.; French morocco, 4s. 6d.; calf, 7s. 6d. No. 3, bound with the Psalms and Paraphrases, cloth, 2s.; French morocco, 3s.

―――― The Scottish Hymnal, with Music. Selected by the Committees on Hymns and on Psalmody. The harmonies arranged by W. H. Monk. Cloth, 1s. 6d.; French morocco, 3s. 6d. The same in the Tonic Sol-fa Notation, 1s. 6d. and 3s. 6d.

GERARD. Reata: What's in a Name? By E. D. GERARD. New Edition. In one volume, crown 8vo. [Nearly ready.

GLEIG. The Subaltern. By G. R. GLEIG, M.A., late Chaplain-General of her Majesty's Forces. Originally published in 'Blackwood's Magazine.' Library Edition. Revised and Corrected, with a New Preface. Crown 8vo, 7s. 6d.

GOETHE'S FAUST. Translated into English Verse by Sir THEODORE MARTIN, K.C.B. Second Edition, post 8vo, 6s. Cheap Edition, fcap., 3s. 6d.

―――― Poems and Ballads of Goethe. Translated by Professor AYTOUN and Sir THEODORE MARTIN, K.C.B. Third Edition, fcap. 8vo, 6s.

GORDON CUMMING. At Home in Fiji. By C. F. GORDON CUMMING, Author of 'From the Hebrides to the Himalayas.' 2 vols. 8vo. With Illustrations and Map. 25s.

GRAHAM. Annals and Correspondence of the Viscount and First and Second Earls of Stair. By JOHN MURRAY GRAHAM. 2 vols. demy 8vo, with Portraits and other Illustrations. £1, 8s.

―――― Memoir of Lord Lynedoch. Second Edition, crown 8vo, 5s.

GRANT. Bush-Life in Queensland. By A. C. GRANT. In 2 vols. post 8vo.

GRANT. Incidents in the Sepoy War of 1857-58. Compiled from the Private Journals of the late General Sir HOPE GRANT, G.C.B.; together with some Explanatory Chapters by Captain HENRY KNOLLYS, R.A. Crown 8vo, with Map and Plans, 12s.

GRANT. Memorials of the Castle of Edinburgh. By JAMES GRANT. A New Edition. Crown 8vo, with 12 Engravings, 2s.

HAMERTON. Wenderholme: A Story of Lancashire and Yorkshire Life. By PHILIP GILBERT HAMERTON, Author of 'A Painter's Camp.' A New Edition. Crown 8vo, 6s.

HAMILTON. Lectures on Metaphysics. By Sir WILLIAM HAMILTON, Bart., Professor of Logic and Metaphysics in the University of Edinburgh. Edited by the Rev. H. L. MANSEL, B.D., LL.D., Dean of St Paul's; and JOHN VEITCH, M.A., Professor of Logic and Rhetoric, Glasgow. Sixth Edition. 2 vols. 8vo, 24s.

——— Lectures on Logic. Edited by the SAME. Third Edition. 2 vols. 24s.

——— Discussions on Philosophy and Literature, Education and University Reform. Third Edition. 8vo, 21s.

——— Memoir of Sir William Hamilton, Bart., Professor of Logic and Metaphysics in the University of Edinburgh. By Professor VEITCH of the University of Glasgow. 8vo, with Portrait, 18s.

HAMILTON. Annals of the Peninsular Campaigns. By Captain THOMAS HAMILTON. Edited by F. Hardman. 8vo, 16s. Atlas of Maps to illustrate the Campaigns, 12s.

HAMLEY. The Operations of War Explained and Illustrated. By Sir EDWARD BRUCE HAMLEY, C.B. Fourth Edition, revised throughout. 4to, with numerous Illustrations, 30s.

——— Thomas Carlyle: An Essay. Second Edition. Crown 8vo. 2s. 6d.

——— The Story of the Campaign of Sebastopol. Written in the Camp. With Illustrations drawn in Camp by the Author. 8vo, 21s.

——— On Outposts. Second Edition. 8vo, 2s.

——— Wellington's Career; A Military and Political Summary. Crown 8vo, 2s.

——— Lady Lee's Widowhood. Crown 8vo, 2s. 6d.

——— Our Poor Relations. A Philozoic Essay. With Illustrations, chiefly by Ernest Griset. Crown 8vo, cloth gilt, 3s. 6d.

HAMLEY. Guilty, or Not Guilty? A Tale. By Major-General W. G. HAMLEY, late of the Royal Engineers. New Edition. Crown 8vo, 3s. 6d.

——— The House of Lys: One Book of its History. A Tale. Second Edition. 2 vols. crown 8vo. 17s.

HANDY HORSE-BOOK; or, Practical Instructions in Riding, Driving, and the General Care and Management of Horses. By 'MAGENTA.' Ninth Edition, with 6 Engravings, 4s. 6d.

BY THE SAME.

Our Domesticated Dogs: their Treatment in reference to Food, Diseases, Habits, Punishment, Accomplishments. Crown 8vo, 2s. 6d.

HARBORD. A Glossary of Navigation. Containing the Definitions and Propositions of the Science, Explanation of Terms, and Description of Instruments. By the Rev. J. B. HARBORD, M.A., Assistant Director of Education, Admiralty. Crown 8vo. Illustrated with Diagrams, 6s.

——— Definitions and Diagrams in Astronomy and Navigation. 1s.

——— Short Sermons for Hospitals and Sick Seamen. Fcap. 8vo, cloth, 4s. 6d.

HARDMAN. Scenes and Adventures in Central America. Edited by FREDERICK HARDMAN. Crown 8vo, 6s.

HAWKEY. The Shakespeare Tapestry. Woven in Verse. By C. HAWKEY. Fcap. 8vo. 6s.

HAY. The Works of the Right Rev. Dr George Hay, Bishop of Edinburgh. Edited under the Supervision of the Right Rev. Bishop STRAIN. With Memoir and Portrait of the Author. 5 vols. crown 8vo, bound in extra cloth, £1, 1s. Or, sold separately—viz. :

——— The Sincere Christian Instructed in the Faith of Christ from the Written Word. 2 vols., 8s.

——— The Devout Christian Instructed in the Law of Christ from the Written Word. 2 vols., 8s.

——— The Pious Christian Instructed in the Nature and Practice of the Principal Exercises of Piety. 1 vol., 4s.

HEMANS. The Poetical Works of Mrs Hemans. Copyright Editions.
One Volume, royal 8vo, 5s.
The Same, with Illustrations engraved on Steel, bound in cloth, gilt edges, 7s. 6d.
Six Volumes, fcap., 12s. 6d.
Seven Volumes, fcap., with Memoir by her SISTER. 35s.
SELECT POEMS OF MRS HEMANS. Fcap., cloth, gilt edges, 3s.

——— Memoir of Mrs Hemans. By her SISTER. With a Portrait, fcap. 8vo, 5s.

HOLE. A Book about Roses: How to Grow and Show Them. By the Rev. Canon HOLE. With coloured Frontispiece by the Hon. Mrs Francklin. Seventh Edition, revised. Crown 8vo, 7s. 6d.

HOME PRAYERS. By Ministers of the Church of Scotland and Members of the Church Service Society. Fcap. 8vo, price 3s.

HOMER. The Odyssey. Translated into English Verse in the Spenserian Stanza. By PHILIP STANHOPE WORSLEY. Third Edition, 2 vols., fcap., 12s.

——— The Iliad. Translated by P. S. WORSLEY and Professor CONINGTON. 2 vols. crown 8vo, 21s.

HOSACK. Mary Queen of Scots and Her Accusers. Containing a Variety of Documents never before published. By JOHN HOSACK, Barrister-at-Law. A New and Enlarged Edition, with a Photograph from the Bust on the Tomb in Westminster Abbey. 2 vols. 8vo, £1, 1s.

INDEX GEOGRAPHICUS : Being a List, alphabetically arranged, of the Principal Places on the Globe, with the Countries and Subdivisions of the Countries in which they are situated, and their Latitudes and Longitudes. Applicable to all Modern Atlases and Maps. Imperial 8vo, pp. 676, 21s.

JEAN JAMBON. Our Trip to Blunderland ; or, Grand Excursion to Blundertown and Back. By JEAN JAMBON. With Sixty Illustrations designed by CHARLES DOYLE, engraved by DALZIEL. Fourth Thousand. Handsomely bound in cloth, gilt edges, 6s. 6d. Cheap Edition, cloth, 3s. 6d. In boards, 2s. 6d.

JOHNSON. The Scots Musical Museum. Consisting of upwards of Six Hundred Songs, with proper Basses for the Pianoforte. Originally published by JAMES JOHNSON ; and now accompanied with Copious Notes and Illustrations of the Lyric Poetry and Music of Scotland, by the late WILLIAM STENHOUSE ; with additional Notes and Illustrations, by DAVID LAING and C. K. SHARPE. 4 vols. 8vo, Roxburghe binding, £2, 12s. 6d.

JOHNSTON. The Chemistry of Common Life. By Professor J. F. W. JOHNSTON. New Edition, Revised, and brought down to date. By ARTHUR HERBERT CHURCH, M.A. Oxon.; Author of 'Food: its Sources, Constituents, and Uses;' 'The Laboratory Guide for Agricultural Students;' 'Plain Words about Water,' &c. Illustrated with Maps and 102 Engravings on Wood. Complete in One Volume, crown 8vo, pp. 618, 7s. 6d.

——— Professor Johnston's Elements of Agricultural Chemistry and Geology. Twelfth Edition, Revised, and brought down to date. By CHARLES A. CAMERON, M.D., F.R.C.S.I., &c. Fcap. 8vo, 6s. 6d.

——— Catechism of Agricultural Chemistry and Geology. An entirely New Edition, revised and enlarged, by CHARLES A. CAMERON, M.D., F.R.C.S.I., &c. Seventy-eighth Thousand, with numerous Illustrations, 1s.

——— Notes on North America: Agricultural, Economical, and Social. 2 vols. post 8vo, 21s.

KING. The Metamorphoses of Ovid. Translated in English Blank Verse. By HENRY KING, M.A., Fellow of Wadham College, Oxford, and of the Inner Temple, Barrister-at-Law. Crown 8vo, 10s. 6d.

KINGLAKE. History of the Invasion of the Crimea. By A. W. KINGLAKE. Cabinet Edition. Six Volumes, crown 8vo, at 6s. each. The Volumes respectively contain:—

   I. THE ORIGIN OF THE WAR between the Czar and the Sultan.
   II. RUSSIA MET AND INVADED. With 4 Maps and Plans.
   III. THE BATTLE OF THE ALMA. With 14 Maps and Plans.
   IV. SEBASTOPOL AT BAY. With 10 Maps and Plans.
   V. THE BATTLE OF BALACLAVA. With 10 Maps and Plans.
   VI. THE BATTLE OF INKERMAN. With 11 Maps and Plans.

——— History of the Invasion of the Crimea. Vol. VI. Winter Troubles. Demy 8vo, with a Map, 16s.

——— Eothen. A New Edition, uniform with the Cabinet Edition of the 'History of the Crimean War,' price 6s.

KNOLLYS. The Elements of Field-Artillery. Designed for the Use of Infantry and Cavalry Officers. By HENRY KNOLLYS, Captain Royal Artillery; Author of 'From Sedan to Saarbrück,' Editor of 'Incidents in the Sepoy War,' &c. With Engravings. Crown 8vo, 7s. 6d.

LAKEMAN. What I saw in Kaffir-land. By Sir STEPHEN LAKEMAN (MAZHAR PACHA). Post 8vo, 8s. 6d.

LAVERGNE. The Rural Economy of England, Scotland, and Ireland. By LEONCE DE LAVERGNE. Translated from the French. With Notes by a Scottish Farmer. 8vo, 12s.

LEE. Lectures on the History of the Church of Scotland, from the Reformation to the Revolution Settlement. By the late Very Rev. JOHN LEE, D.D., LL.D., Principal of the University of Edinburgh. With Notes and Appendices from the Author's Papers. Edited by the Rev. WILLIAM LEE, D.D. 2 vols. 8vo, 21s.

LEE-HAMILTON. Poems and Transcripts. By EUGENE LEE-HAMILTON. Crown 8vo, 6s.

LEWES. The Physiology of Common Life. By GEORGE H. LEWES, Author of 'Sea-side Studies,' &c. Illustrated with numerous Engravings. 2 vols., 12s.

LOCKHART. Doubles and Quits. By Laurence W. M. Lockhart. With Twelve Illustrations. Third Edition. Crown 8vo, 6s.

——— Fair to See : a Novel. Sixth Edition, crown 8vo, 6s.

——— Mine is Thine : a Novel. Sixth Edition, crown 8vo, 6s.

LORIMER. The Institutes of Law : A Treatise of the Principles of Jurisprudence as determined by Nature. By James Lorimer, Regius Professor of Public Law and of the Law of Nature and Nations in the University of Edinburgh. New Edition, revised throughout, and much enlarged. 8vo, 18s.

LYON. History of the Rise and Progress of Freemasonry in Scotland. By David Murray Lyon, Secretary to the Grand Lodge of Scotland. In small quarto. Illustrated with numerous Portraits of Eminent Members of the Craft, and Facsimiles of Ancient Charters and other Curious Documents. £1, 11s. 6d.

M'COMBIE. Cattle and Cattle-Breeders. By William M'Combie, Tillyfour. A New and Cheaper Edition, 2s. 6d., cloth.

MACRAE. A Handbook of Deer-Stalking. By Alexander Macrae, late Forester to Lord Henry Bentinck. With Introduction by Horatio Ross, Esq. Fcap. 8vo, with two Photographs from Life. 3s. 6d.

M'CRIE. Works of the Rev. Thomas M'Crie, D.D. Uniform Edition. Four vols. crown 8vo, 24s

——— Life of John Knox. Containing Illustrations of the History of the Reformation in Scotland. Crown 8vo, 6s. Another Edition, 3s. 6d.

——— Life of Andrew Melville. Containing Illustrations of the Ecclesiastical and Literary History of Scotland in the Sixteenth and Seventeenth Centuries. Crown 8vo, 6s.

——— History of the Progress and Suppression of the Reformation in Italy in the Sixteenth Century. Crown 8vo, 4s.

——— History of the Progress and Suppression of the Reformation in Spain in the Sixteenth Century. Crown 8vo, 3s. 6d.

——— Sermons, and Review of the 'Tales of My Landlord.' Crown 8vo, 6s.

——— Lectures on the Book of Esther. Fcap. 8vo, 5s.

M'INTOSH. The Book of the Garden. By Charles M'Intosh, formerly Curator of the Royal Gardens of his Majesty the King of the Belgians, and lately of those of his Grace the Duke of Buccleuch, K.G., at Dalkeith Palace. Two large vols. royal 8vo, embellished with 1350 Engravings. £4, 7s. 6d.
Vol. I. On the Formation of Gardens and Construction of Garden Edifices. 776 pages, and 1073 Engravings, £2, 10s.
Vol. II. Practical Gardening. 868 pages, and 279 Engravings, £1, 17s. 6d.

MACKAY. A Manual of Modern Geography ; Mathematical, Physical, and Political. By the Rev. Alexander Mackay, LL.D , F.R.G.S. New and Greatly Improved Edition. Crown 8vo, pp. 688 7s. 6d.

——— Elements of Modern Geography. 46th Thousand, revised to the present time. Crown 8vo, pp. 300, 3s.

——— The Intermediate Geography. Intended as an Intermediate Book between the Author's 'Outlines of Geography,' and 'Elements of Geography.' Sixth Edition, crown 8vo, pp. 224, 2s.

——— Outlines of Modern Geography. 131st Thousand, revised to the Present Time. 18mo, pp. 112, 1s.

——— First Steps in Geography. 69th Thousand. 18mo, pp. 56. Sewed, 4d.; cloth, 6d.

——— Elements of Physiography and Physical Geography. With Express Reference to the Instructions recently Issued by the Science and Art Department. 15th Thousand. Crown 8vo, 1s. 6d.

MACKAY. Facts and Dates; or, the Leading Events in Sacred and Profane History, and the Principal Facts in the various Physical Sciences. The Memory being aided throughout by a Simple and Natural Method. For Schools and Private Reference. New Edition, thoroughly Revised. Crown 8vo, 3s. 6d.

MACKENZIE. Studies in Roman Law. With Comparative Views of the Laws of France, England, and Scotland. By LORD MACKENZIE, one of the Judges of the Court of Session in Scotland. Fifth Edition, Edited by JOHN KIRKPATRICK, Esq., M.A. Cantab.; Dr Jur. Heidelb.; LL.B., Edin.; Advocate. 8vo, 12s.

MANNERS. Notes of an Irish Tour in 1846. By Lord JOHN MANNERS, M.P., G.C.B. New Edition, crown 8vo. 2s. 6d.

MARMORNE. The Story is told by ADOLPHUS SEGRAVE, the youngest of three Brothers. Third Edition. Crown 8vo. 6s.

MARSHALL. French Home Life. By FREDERIC MARSHALL. CONTENTS: Servants.—Children.—Furniture.—Food.—Manners.—Language.—Dress. —Marriage. Second Edition. 5s.

MARSHMAN. History of India. From the Earliest Period to the Close of the India Company's Government; with an Epitome of Subsequent Events. By JOHN CLARK MARSHMAN, C.S I. Abridged from the Author's larger work. Second Edition, revised. Crown 8vo, with Map, 6s. 6d.

MARTIN. Goethe's Faust. Translated by Sir THEODORE MARTIN, K.C.B. Second Edition, crown 8vo, 6s. Cheap Edition, 3s. 6d.

——— The Works of Horace. Translated into English Verse, with Life and Notes. Fourth Edition. In 2 vols. crown 8vo, printed on hand-made paper. [*In the press.*

——— Poems and Ballads of Heinrich Heine. Done into English Verse. Printed on *papier vergé*, crown 8vo, 8s.

——— Catullus. With Life and Notes. Second Edition, post 8vo, 7s. 6d.

——— The Vita Nuova of Dante. With an Introduction and Notes. Second Edition, crown 8vo, 5s.

——— Aladdin: A Dramatic Poem. By ADAM OEHLENSCHLAEGER. Fcap. 8vo, 5s.

——— Correggio: A Tragedy. By OEHLENSCHLAEGER. With Notes. Fcap. 8vo, 3s.

——— King Rene's Daughter: A Danish Lyrical Drama. By HENRIK HERTZ. Second Edition, fcap., 2s. 6d.

MEIKLEJOHN. An Old Educational Reformer—Dr Bell. By J. M D. MEIKLEJOHN, M.A., Professor of the Theory, History, and Practice of Education in the University of St Andrews. Crown 8vo, 3s. 6d.

MINTO. A Manual of English Prose Literature, Biographical and Critical; designed mainly to show Characteristics of Style. By W. MINTO, M.A., Professor of Logic in the University of Aberdeen. Second Edition, revised. Crown 8vo, 7s. 6d.

——— Characteristics of English Poets, from Chaucer to Shirley. Crown 8vo, 9s.

MITCHELL. Biographies of Eminent Soldiers of the last Four Centuries. By Major-General JOHN MITCHELL, Author of 'Life of Wallenstein.' With a Memoir of the Author. 8vo, 9s.

MOIR. Poetical Works of D. M. MOIR (Delta). With Memoir by THOMAS AIRD, and Portrait. Second Edition, 2 vols. fcap. 8vo, 12s.

—— Domestic Verses. New Edition, fcap. 8vo, cloth gilt, 4s. 6d.

—— Lectures on the Poetical Literature of the Past Half-Century. Third Edition, fcap. 8vo, 5s.

—— Life of Mansie Wauch, Tailor in Dalkeith. With 8 Illustrations on Steel, by the late GEORGE CRUIKSHANK. Crown 8vo. 3s. 6d. Another Edition, fcap. 8vo, 1s. 6d.

MONTAGUE. Campaigning in South Africa. Reminiscences of an Officer in 1879. By Captain W. E. MONTAGUE, 94th Regiment, Author of 'Claude Meadowleigh,' &c. 8vo, 10s. 6d.

MONTALEMBERT. Count de Montalembert's History of the Monks of the West. From St Benedict to St Bernard. Translated by Mrs OLIPHANT. 7 vols. 8vo, £3, 17s. 6d.

—— Memoir of Count de Montalembert. A Chapter of Recent French History. By Mrs OLIPHANT, Author of the 'Life of Edward Irving,' &c. 2 vols. crown 8vo. £1, 4s.

MURDOCH. Manual of the Law of Insolvency and Bankruptcy: Comprehending a Summary of the Law of Insolvency, Notour Bankruptcy, Composition-contracts, Trust-deeds, Cession, and Sequestrations; and the Winding-up of Joint-Stock Companies in Scotland; with Annotations on the various Insolvency and Bankruptcy Statutes; and with Forms of Procedure applicable to these Subjects. By JAMES MURDOCH, Member of the Faculty of Procurators in Glasgow. Fourth Edition, Revised and Enlarged, 8vo, £1.

NEAVES. A Glance at some of the Principles of Comparative Philology. As illustrated in the Latin and Anglican Forms of Speech. By the Hon. Lord NEAVES. Crown 8vo, 1s. 6d.

—— Songs and Verses, Social and Scientific. By an Old Contributor to 'Maga.' Fifth Edition, fcap. 8vo, 4s.

—— The Greek Anthology. Being Vol. XX. of 'Ancient Classics for English Readers.' Crown 8vo, 2s. 6d.

NEW VIRGINIANS, THE. By the Author of 'Estelle Russell,' 'Junia,' &c. In 2 vols., post 8vo, 18s.

NICHOLSON. A Manual of Zoology, for the Use of Students. With a General Introduction on the Principles of Zoology. By HENRY ALLEYNE NICHOLSON, M.D., F.R.S.E., F.G.S., &c., Professor of Natural History in the University of St Andrews. Sixth Edition, revised and enlarged. Crown 8vo, pp. 866, with 452 Engravings on Wood, 14s.

—— Text-Book of Zoology, for the Use of Schools. Third Edition, enlarged. Crown 8vo, with 225 Engravings on Wood, 6s.

—— Introductory Text-Book of Zoology, for the Use of Junior Classes. Third Edition, revised and enlarged, with 136 Engravings, 3s.

—— Outlines of Natural History, for Beginners; being Descriptions of a Progressive Series of Zoological Types. Second Edition, with Engravings, 1s. 6d.

NICHOLSON. A Manual of Palæontology, for the Use of Students. With a General Introduction on the Principles of Palæontology. Second Edition. Revised and greatly enlarged. 2 vols. 8vo, with 722 Engravings, £2, 2s.

——— The Ancient Life-History of the Earth. An Outline of the Principles and Leading Facts of Palæontological Science. Crown 8vo, with numerous Engravings, 10s. 6d.

——— On the "Tabulate Corals" of the Palæozoic Period, with Critical Descriptions of Illustrative Species. Illustrated with 15 Lithograph Plates and numerous Engravings. Super-royal 8vo, 21s.

——— On the Structure and Affinities of the Genus Monticulipora and its Sub-Genera, with Critical Descriptions of Illustrative Species. Illustrated with numerous Engravings on wood and lithographed Plates. Super-royal 8vo. 18s.

NICHOLSON. Redeeming the Time, and other Sermons. By the late MAXWELL NICHOLSON, D.D., Minister of St Stephen's, Edinburgh. Crown 8vo, 7s. 6d.

——— Communion with Heaven, and other Sermons. Crown 8vo, 5s. 6d.

——— Rest in Jesus. Sixth Edition. Fcap. 8vo, 4s. 6d.

OLIPHANT. The Land of Gilead. With Excursions in the Lebanon. By LAURENCE OLIPHANT, Author of 'Lord Elgin's Mission to China and Japan,' &c. With Illustrations and Maps. Demy 8vo, 21s.

——— Piccadilly: A Fragment of Contemporary Biography. With Eight Illustrations by Richard Doyle. Fifth Edition, 4s. 6d. Cheap Edition, in paper cover, 2s. 6d.

——— Russian Shores of the Black Sea in the Autumn of 1852. With a Voyage down the Volga and a Tour through the Country of the Don Cossacks. 8vo, with Map and other Illustrations. Fourth Edition, 14s.

OLIPHANT. Historical Sketches of the Reign of George Second. By Mrs OLIPHANT. Third Edition, 6s.

——— The Story of Valentine; and his Brother. 5s., cloth.

——— Katie Stewart. 2s. 6d.

——— Salem Chapel. 2s. 6d., cloth.

——— The Perpetual Curate. 2s. 6d., cloth.

——— Miss Marjoribanks. 2s. 6d., cloth.

——— The Rector, and the Doctor's Family. 1s. 6d., cloth.

——— John: A Love Story. 2s. 6d., cloth.

OSBORN. Narratives of Voyage and Adventure. By Admiral SHERARD OSBORN, C.B. 3 vols. crown 8vo, 12s. Or separately:—

——— Stray Leaves from an Arctic Journal; or, Eighteen Months in the Polar Regions in Search of Sir John Franklin's Expedition in 1850-51. To which is added the Career, Last Voyage, and Fate of Captain Sir John Franklin. New Edition, crown 8vo, 3s. 6d.

——— The Discovery of a North-West Passage by H.M.S. Investigator, during the years 1850-51-52-53-54. Edited from the Logs and Journals of Captain ROBERT C. M'CLURE. Fourth Edition, crown 8vo, 3s. 6d.

——— Quedah; A Cruise in Japanese Waters: and, The Fight on the Peiho. New Edition, crown 8vo, 5s.

OSSIAN. The Poems of Ossian in the Original Gaelic. With a Literal Translation into English, and a Dissertation on the Authenticity of the Poems. By the Rev. ARCHIBALD CLERK. 2 vols. imperial 8vo, £1, 11s. 6d.

PAGE. Introductory Text-Book of Geology. By DAVID PAGE, LL.D., Professor of Geology in the Durham University of Physical Science, Newcastle. With Engravings on Wood and Glossarial Index. Eleventh Edition, 2s. 6d.

——— Advanced Text-Book of Geology, Descriptive and Industrial. With Engravings, and Glossary of Scientific Terms. Sixth Edition, revised and enlarged, 7s. 6d.

——— Handbook of Geological Terms, Geology, and Physical Geography. Second Edition, enlarged, 7s. 6d.

——— Geology for General Readers. A Series of Popular Sketches in Geology and Palæontology. Third Edition, enlarged, 6s.

——— Chips and Chapters. A Book for Amateurs and Young Geologists. 5s.

——— The Past and Present Life of the Globe. With numerous Illustrations. Crown 8vo, 6s.

——— The Crust of the Earth: A Handy Outline of Geology. Sixth Edition, 1s.

——— Economic Geology; or, Geology in its relation to the Arts and Manufactures. With Engravings, and Coloured Map of the British Islands. Crown 8vo, 7s. 6d.

——— Introductory Text-Book of Physical Geography. With Sketch-Maps and Illustrations. Ninth Edition, 2s. 6d.

——— Advanced Text-Book of Physical Geography. Second Edition. With Engravings. 5s.

PAGET. Paradoxes and Puzzles: Historical, Judicial, and Literary. Now for the first time published in Collected Form. By JOHN PAGET, Barrister-at-Law. 8vo, 12s.

PATON. Spindrift. By Sir J. NOEL PATON. Fcap., cloth, 5s.

——— Poems by a Painter. Fcap., cloth, 5s.

PATTERSON. Essays in History and Art. By R. H. PATTERSON. 8vo, 12s.

PAUL. History of the Royal Company of Archers, the Queen's Body-Guard for Scotland. By JAMES BALFOUR PAUL, Advocate of the Scottish Bar. Crown 4to, with Portraits and other Illustrations. £2, 2s.

PAUL. Analysis and Critical Interpretation of the Hebrew Text of the Book of Genesis. Preceded by a Hebrew Grammar, and Dissertations on the Genuineness of the Pentateuch, and on the Structure of the Hebrew Language. By the Rev. WILLIAM PAUL, A.M. 8vo, 18s.

PERSONALITY. The Beginning and End of Metaphysics, and the Necessary Assumption in all Positive Philosophy. Crown 8vo, 3s.

BY THE SAME.

The Origin of Evil, and Other Sermons. Crown 8vo, 4s. 6d.

PETTIGREW. The Handy Book of Bees, and their Profitable Management. By A. PETTIGREW. Fourth Edition, Enlarged, with Engravings. Crown 8vo, 3s. 6d.

PHILOSOPHICAL CLASSICS FOR ENGLISH READERS. Companion Series to Ancient and Foreign Classics for English Readers. Edited by WILLIAM KNIGHT, LL.D., Professor of Moral Philosophy, University of St Andrews. In crown 8vo volumes, with portraits, price 3s. 6d.
1. DESCARTES. By Professor Mahaffy, Dublin.
2. BUTLER. By the Rev. W. Lucas Collins, M.A., Honorary Canon of Peterborough.
3. BERKELEY. By Professor A. Campbell Fraser, Edinburgh.
4. FICHTE. By Professor Adamson, Owen's College, Manchester.

POLLOK. The Course of Time: A Poem. By ROBERT POLLOK, A.M. Small fcap. 8vo, cloth gilt, 2s. 6d. The Cottage Edition, 32mo, sewed, 8d. The Same, cloth, gilt edges, 1s. 6d. Another Edition, with Illustrations by Birket Foster and others, fcap., gilt cloth, 3s. 6d., or with edges gilt, 4s.

PORT ROYAL LOGIC. Translated from the French: with Introduction, Notes, and Appendix. By THOMAS SPENCER BAYNES, LL.D., Professor in the University of St Andrews. Eighth Edition, 12mo, 4s.

POTTS AND DARNELL. Aditus Faciliores: An easy Latin Construing Book, with Complete Vocabulary. By A. W. POTTS, M.A., LL.D., Head-Master of the Fettes College, Edinburgh, and sometime Fellow of St John's College, Cambridge; and the Rev. C. DARNELL, M.A., Head-Master of Cargilfield Preparatory School, Edinburgh, and late Scholar of Pembroke and Downing Colleges, Cambridge. Sixth Edition, fcap. 8vo, 3s. 6d.

——— Aditus Faciliores Graeci. An easy Greek Construing Book, with Complete Vocabulary. Third Edition, fcap. 8vo, 3s.

PRINGLE. The Live-Stock of the Farm. By ROBERT O. PRINGLE. Third Edition, crown 8vo. [In the press.

PUBLIC GENERAL STATUTES AFFECTING SCOTLAND, from 1707 to 1847, with Chronological Table and Index. 3 vols. large 8vo, £3, 3s.

PUBLIC GENERAL STATUTES AFFECTING SCOTLAND, COLLECTION OF. Published Annually with General Index.

RAMSAY. Two Lectures on the Genius of Handel, and the Distinctive Character of his Sacred Compositions. Delivered to the Members of the Edinburgh Philosophical Institution. By the Very Rev. DEAN RAMSAY, Author of 'Reminiscences of Scottish Life and Character.' Crown 8vo, 3s. 6d.

RANKINE. A Treatise on the Rights and Burdens Incident to the Ownership of Lands and other Heritages in Scotland. By JOHN RANKINE, M.A., Advocate. Large 8vo, 40s.

READE. A Woman-Hater. By CHARLES READE. 3 vols. crown 8vo, £1, 5s. 6d. Originally published in 'Blackwood's Magazine.'

REID. A Handy Manual of German Literature. By M. F. REID. For Schools, Civil Service Competitions, and University Local Examinations. Fcap. 8vo, 3s.

ROBERTSON. Orellana, and other Poems. By J. LOGIE ROBERTSON. Fcap. 8vo. Printed on hand-made paper. [In the press.

RUSTOW. The War for the Rhine Frontier, 1870: Its Political and Military History. By Col. W. RUSTOW. Translated from the German, by JOHN LAYLAND NEEDHAM, Lieutenant R.M. Artillery. 3 vols. 8vo, with Maps and Plans, £1, 11s. 6d.

ST STEPHENS; or, Illustrations of Parliamentary Oratory. A Poem. Comprising—Pym—Vane—Strafford—Halifax—Shaftesbury—St John—Sir R. Walpole—Chesterfield—Carteret—Chatham—Pitt—Fox—Burke—Sheridan—Wilberforce—Wyndham—Conway—Castlereagh—William Lamb (Lord Melbourne)—Tierney—Lord Gray—O'Connell—Plunkett—Shiel—Follett—Macaulay—Peel. Second Edition, crown 8vo, 5s.

SANDFORD AND TOWNSEND. The Great Governing Families of England. By J. LANGTON SANDFORD and MEREDITH TOWNSEND. 2 vols. 8vo, 15s., in extra binding, with richly-gilt cover.

SCHETKY. Ninety Years of Work and Play. Sketches from the Public and Private Career of JOHN CHRISTIAN SCHETKY, late Marine Painter in Ordinary to the Queen. By his DAUGHTER. Crown 8vo, 7s. 6d.

SCOTTISH NATURALIST, THE. A Quarterly Magazine of Natural History. Edited by F. BUCHANAN WHITE, M.D., F.L S. Annual Subscription, free by post, 4s.

SELLAR. Manual of the Education Acts for Scotland. By ALEXANDER CRAIG SELLAR, Advocate. Seventh Edition, greatly enlarged, and revised to the present time. 8vo, 15s.

SELLER AND STEPHENS. Physiology at the Farm; in Aid of Rearing and Feeding the Live Stock. By WILLIAM SELLER, M.D., F.R.S.E., Fellow of the Royal College of Physicians, Edinburgh, formerly Lecturer on Materia Medica and Dietetics; and HENRY STEPHENS, F.R.S.E., Author of 'The Book of the Farm,' &c. Post 8vo, with Engravings, 16s.

SETON. St Kilda: Past and Present. By GEORGE SETON, M.A. Oxon.; Author of the 'Law and Practice of Heraldry in Scotland,' &c. With appropriate Illustrations. Small quarto, 15s.

SHADWELL. The Life of Colin Campbell, Lord Clyde. Illustrated by Extracts from his Diary and Correspondence. By Lieutenant-General SHADWELL, C.B. 2 vols. 8vo. With Portrait, Maps, and Plans. 36s.

SIMPSON. Paris after Waterloo: A Revised Edition of a "Visit to Flanders and the Field of Waterloo." By JAMES SIMPSON, Advocate. With 2 coloured Plans of the Battle. Crown 8vo, 5s.

SMITH. Italian Irrigation: A Report on the Agricultural Canals of Piedmont and Lombardy, addressed to the Hon. the Directors of the East India Company; with an Appendix, containing a Sketch of the Irrigation System of Northern and Central India. By Lieut.-Col. R. BAIRD SMITH, F.G S., Captain, Bengal Engineers. Second Edition. 2 vols. 8vo, with Atlas in folio, 30s.

SMITH. Thorndale; or, The Conflict of Opinions. By WILLIAM SMITH, Author of 'A Discourse on Ethics,' &c. A New Edition. Crown 8vo, 10s. 6d.

—— Gravenhurst; or, Thoughts on Good and Evil. Second Edition, with Memoir of the Author. Crown 8vo, 8s.

—— A Discourse on Ethics of the School of Paley. 8vo, 4s.

—— Dramas. 1. Sir William Crichton. 2. Athelwold. 3. Guidone. 24mo, boards, 3s.

SOUTHEY. Poetical Works of Caroline Bowles Southey. Fcap. 8vo, 5s.

—— The Birthday, and other Poems. Second Edition, 5s.

—— Chapters on Churchyards. Fcap., 2s. 6d.

SPEKE. What led to the Discovery of the Nile Source. By JOHN HANNING SPEKE, Captain H.M. Indian Army. 8vo, with Maps, &c., 14s.

—— Journal of the Discovery of the Source of the Nile. By J. H. SPEKE, Captain H M. Indian Army. With a Map of Eastern Equatorial Africa by Captain SPEKE; numerous illustrations, chiefly from Drawings by Captain GRANT; and Portraits, engraved on Steel, of Captains SPEKE and GRANT. 8vo. 21s.

STARFORTH. Villa Residences and Farm Architecture: A Series of Designs. By JOHN STARFORTH, Architect. 102 Engravings. Second Edition, medium 4to, £2, 17s. 6d.

STATISTICAL ACCOUNT OF SCOTLAND. Complete, with Index, 15 vols. 8vo, £16, 16s.
Each County sold separately, with Title, Index, and Map, neatly bound in cloth, forming a very valuable Manual to the Landowner, the Tenant, the Manufacturer, the Naturalist, the Tourist, &c.

STEPHENS. The Book of the Farm; detailing the Labours of the Farmer, Farm-Steward, Ploughman, Shepherd, Hedger, Farm-Labourer, Field-Worker, and Cattleman. By HENRY STEPHENS, F.R.S.E. Illustrated with Portraits of Animals painted from the life; and with 557 Engravings on Wood, representing the principal Field Operations, Implements, and Animals treated of in the Work. A New and Revised Edition, the third, in great part Rewritten. 2 vols. large 8vo, £2, 10s.

——— The Book of Farm-Buildings; their Arrangement and Construction. By HENRY STEPHENS, F.R.S.E., Author of 'The Book of the Farm;' and ROBERT SCOTT BURN. Illustrated with 1045 Plates and Engravings. Large 8vo, uniform with 'The Book of the Farm,' &c. £1, 11s. 6d.

——— The Book of Farm Implements and Machines. By J. SLIGHT and R. SCOTT BURN, Engineers. Edited by HENRY STEPHENS. Large 8vo, uniform with 'The Book of the Farm,' £2, 2s.

——— Catechism of Practical Agriculture. With Engravings. 1s.

STEWART. Advice to Purchasers of Horses. By JOHN STEWART, V.S. Author of 'Stable Economy.' 2s. 6d.

——— Stable Economy. A Treatise on the Management of Horses in relation to Stabling, Grooming, Feeding, Watering, and Working. Seventh Edition, fcap. 8vo, 6s. 6d.

STIRLING. Missing Proofs: a Pembrokeshire Tale. By M. C. STIRLING, Author of 'The Grahams of Invermoy.' 2 vols. crown 8vo.
[In the press.

STORMONTH. Etymological and Pronouncing Dictionary of the English Language. Including a very Copious Selection of Scientific Terms. For Use in Schools and Colleges, and as a Book of General Reference. By the Rev. JAMES STORMONTH. The Pronunciation carefully Revised by the Rev. P. H. PHELP, M.A. Cantab. Sixth Edition, with enlarged Supplement, containing many words not to be found in any other Dictionary. Crown 8vo, pp. 800. 7s. 6d.

——— The School Etymological Dictionary and Word-Book. Combining the advantages of an ordinary pronouncing School Dictionary and an Etymological Spelling-book. Fcap. 8vo, pp. 254. 2s.

STORY. Graffiti D'Italia. By W. W. STORY, Author of 'Roba di Roma.' Second Edition, fcap. 8vo, 7s. 6d.

——— Nero; A Historical Play. Fcap. 8vo, 6s.

——— Vallombrosa. Post 8vo.

STRICKLAND. Lives of the Queens of Scotland, and English Princesses connected with the Regal Succession of Great Britain. By AGNES STRICKLAND. With Portraits and Historical Vignettes. 8 vols. post 8vo, £4, 4s.

STURGIS. John-a-Dreams. A Tale. By JULIAN STURGIS. New Edition, crown 8vo, 3s. 6d.

——— An Accomplished Gentleman. Second Edition. Post 8vo, 7s. 6d.

SUTHERLAND. Handbook of Hardy Herbaceous and Alpine Flowers, for general Garden Decoration. Containing Descriptions, in Plain Language, of upwards of 1000 Species of Ornamental Hardy Perennial and Alpine Plants, adapted to all classes of Flower-Gardens, Rockwork, and Waters; along with Concise and Plain Instructions for their Propagation and Culture. By WILLIAM SUTHERLAND, Gardener to the Earl of Minto; formerly Manager of the Herbaceous Department at Kew. Crown 8vo, 7s. 6d.

SWAINSON. A Handbook of Weather Folk-Lore. Being a Collection of Proverbial Sayings in various Languages relating to the Weather, with Explanatory and Illustrative Notes. By the Rev. C. SWAINSON, M.A., Vicar of High Hurst Wood. Fcap. 8vo, Roxburghe binding, 6s. 6d.

SWAYNE. Lake Victoria: A Narrative of Explorations in Search of the Source of the Nile. Compiled from the Memoirs of Captains Speke and Grant. By GEORGE C. SWAYNE, M.A., late Fellow of Corpus Christi College, Oxford. Illustrated with Woodcuts and Map. Crown 8vo, 7s. 6d.

TAYLOR. Destruction and Reconstruction: Personal Experiences of the Late War in the United States. By RICHARD TAYLOR, Lieutenant-General in the Confederate Army. 8vo, 10s. 6d.

TAYLOR. The Story of My Life. By the late Colonel MEADOWS TAYLOR, Author of 'The Confessions of a Thug,' &c. &c. Edited by his Daughter. Third Edition, post 8vo, 9s.

THOLUCK. Hours of Christian Devotion. Translated from the German of A. Tholuck, D.D., Professor of Theology in the University of Halle. By the Rev. ROBERT MENZIES, D.D. With a Preface written for this Translation by the Author. Second Edition, crown 8vo, 7s. 6d.

THOMSON. Handy Book of the Flower-Garden: being Practical Directions for the Propagation, Culture, and Arrangement of Plants in Flower-Gardens all the year round. Embracing all classes of Gardens, from the largest to the smallest. With Engraved and Coloured Plans, illustrative of the various systems of Grouping in Beds and Borders. By DAVID THOMSON, Gardener to his Grace the Duke of Buccleuch, K.G., at Drumlanrig. Third Edition, crown 8vo, 7s. 6d.

——— The Handy Book of Fruit-Culture under Glass: being a series of Elaborate Practical Treatises on the Cultivation and Forcing of Pines, Vines, Peaches, Figs, Melons, Strawberries, and Cucumbers. With Engravings of Hothouses, &c., most suitable for the Cultivation and Forcing of these Fruits. Crown 8vo, with Engravings, 7s. 6d.

THOMSON. A Practical Treatise on the Cultivation of the Grape-Vine. By WILLIAM THOMSON, Tweed Vineyards. Ninth Edition, 8vo, 5s.

TOM CRINGLE'S LOG. A New Edition, with Illustrations. Crown 8vo, cloth gilt, 5s. Cheap Edition, 2s.

TRANSACTIONS OF THE HIGHLAND AND AGRICULTURAL SOCIETY OF SCOTLAND. Published annually, price 5s.

TULLOCH. Rational Theology and Christian Philosophy in England in the Seventeenth Century. By JOHN TULLOCH, D.D., Principal of St Mary's College in the University of St Andrews; and one of her Majesty's Chaplains in Ordinary in Scotland. Second Edition. 2 vols. 8vo, 28s.

——— Some Facts of Religion and of Life. Sermons Preached before her Majesty the Queen in Scotland, 1866-76. Second Edition, crown 8vo, 7s. 6d.

TULLOCH. The Christian Doctrine of Sin; being the Croall Lecture for 1876. Crown 8vo, 6s.

——— Theism. The Witness of Reason and Nature to an All-Wise and Beneficent Creator. 8vo, 10s. 6d.

TYTLER. The Wonder-Seeker; or, The History of Charles Douglas. By M. FRASER TYTLER, Author of 'Tales of the Great and Brave,' &c. A New Edition. Fcap., 3s. 6d.

VIRGIL. The Æneid of Virgil. Translated in English Blank Verse by G. K. RICKARDS, M.A., and Lord RAVENSWORTH. 2 vols. fcap. 8vo, 10s.

WALFORD. Mr Smith: A Part of his Life. By L. B. WALFORD. Cheap Edition, 3s. 6d.

——— Pauline. Fifth Edition. Crown 8vo, 6s.

——— Cousins. Cheaper Edition. Crown 8vo, 6s.

——— Troublesome Daughters. Cheaper Edition. Crown 8vo, 6s.

WARREN'S (SAMUEL) WORKS. People's Edition, 4 vols. crown 8vo, cloth, 18s. Or separately:—

Diary of a Late Physician. 3s. 6d. Illustrated, crown 8vo, 7s. 6d.

Ten Thousand A-Year. 5s.

Now and Then. The Lily and the Bee. Intellectual and Moral Development of the Present Age. 4s. 6d.

Essays: Critical, Imaginative, and Juridical. 5s.

WARREN. The Five Books of the Psalms. With Marginal Notes. By Rev. SAMUEL L. WARREN, Rector of Esher, Surrey; late Fellow, Dean, and Divinity Lecturer, Wadham College, Oxford. Crown 8vo, 5s.

WELLINGTON. Wellington Prize Essays on "the System of Field Manœuvres best adapted for enabling our Troops to meet a Continental Army." Edited by Sir EDWARD BRUCE HAMLEY, C.B. 8vo, 12s. 6d.

WESTMINSTER ASSEMBLY. Minutes of the Westminster Assembly, while engaged in preparing their Directory for Church Government, Confession of Faith, and Catechisms (November 1644 to March 1649). Printed from Transcripts of the Originals procured by the General Assembly of the Church of Scotland. Edited by the Rev. ALEX. T. MITCHELL, D.D., Professor of Ecclesiastical History in the University of St Andrews, and the Rev. JOHN STRUTHERS, LL.D., Minister of Prestonpans. With a Historical and Critical Introduction by Professor Mitchell. 8vo, 15s.

WHITE. The Eighteen Christian Centuries. By the Rev. JAMES WHITE, Author of 'The History of France.' Seventh Edition, post 8vo, with Index, 6s.

——— History of France, from the Earliest Times. Sixth Thousand, post 8vo, with Index, 6s.

WHITE. Archæological Sketches in Scotland—Kintyre and Knapdale. By Captain T. P. WHITE, R.E., of the Ordnance Survey. With numerous Illustrations. 2 vols. folio, £4, 4s. Vol. I., Kintyre, sold separately, £2, 2s.

WILLS AND GREENE. Drawing-room Dramas for Children. By W. G. WILLS and the Hon. Mrs GREENE. Crown 8vo, 6s.

WILSON. The "Ever-Victorious Army:" A History of the Chinese Campaign under Lieut.-Col. C. G. Gordon, and of the Suppression of the Tai-ping Rebellion. By ANDREW WILSON, F.A.S.L. 8vo, with Maps, 15s.

——— The Abode of Snow: Observations on a Journey from Chinese Tibet to the Indian Caucasus, through the Upper Valleys of the Himalaya. New Edition. Crown 8vo, with Map, 10s. 6d.

WILSON. Works of Professor Wilson. Edited by his Son-in-Law, Professor FERRIER. 12 vols. crown 8vo, £2, 8s.

——— Christopher in his Sporting-Jacket. 2 vols., 8s.

——— Isle of Palms, City of the Plague, and other Poems. 4s.

——— Lights and Shadows of Scottish Life, and other Tales. 4s.

——— Essays, Critical and Imaginative. 4 vols., 16s.

——— The Noctes Ambrosianæ. Complete, 4 vols., 14s.

——— The Comedy of the Noctes Ambrosianæ. By CHRISTOPHER NORTH. Edited by JOHN SKELTON, Advocate. With a Portrait of Professor Wilson and of the Ettrick Shepherd, engraved on Steel. Crown 8vo, 7s. 6d.

——— Homer and his Translators, and the Greek Drama. Crown 8vo, 4s.

WINGATE. Annie Weir, and other Poems. By DAVID WINGATE. Fcap. 8vo, 5s.

——— Lily Neil. A Poem. Crown 8vo, 4s. 6d.

WORSLEY. Poems and Translations. By PHILIP STANHOPE WORSLEY, M.A. Edited by EDWARD WORSLEY. Second Edition, enlarged. Fcap. 8vo, 6s.

WYLDE. A Dreamer. By KATHARINE WYLDE. In 3 vols., post 8vo, 25s. 6d.

YOUNG. Songs of Béranger done into English Verse. By WILLIAM YOUNG. New Edition, revised. Fcap. 8vo, 4s. 6d.

YULE. Fortification: for the Use of Officers in the Army, and Readers of Military History. By Col. YULE, Bengal Engineers. 8vo, with numerous Illustrations, 10s. 6d.

www.ingramcontent.com/pod-product-compliance
Lightning Source LLC
Chambersburg PA
CBHW030816230426
43667CB00008B/1247